ON BEING FIT TO LIVE WITH

Other Books
by

HARRY EMERSON FOSDICK

o

o

On Being Fit To Live With

Sermons on Post-War Christianity

by

HARRY EMERSON FOSDICK

PUBLISHERS
HARPER & BROTHERS
NEW YORK AND LONDON

Contents

CONTENTS

Introduction

THESE sermons spring from and deal with the conditions we face following the second World War. They are presented with no endeavor to conceal, in style or structure, the fact that they were spoken discourse. If, therefore, they are to be understood, they must be read with the eye, as though they were being listened to with the ear.

Sermons were not meant to be read, as essays are. The dominant factor in an essay is the *subject* to be elucidated; the dominant factor in a sermon is the *object* to be attained. A good sermon is direct personal address, individual consultation on a group scale, intended to achieve results. A sermon should creatively get things done, then and there, in the minds and lives of the audience; it should be a convincing appeal to a listening jury for decision. If a printed sermon is to seem real, therefore, the reader must read as though he were listening.

Moreover, sermons spring out of immediate occasions. The basic truths they present may be eternal, but the situations they deal with, the personal moods, attitudes and temptations they are meant to meet, are contemporary. In a year whose rapidly shifting scene is so full of fugitive events, therefore, one publishes a volume of sermons with humility. Before the first readers get at the book, many of the situations that called out the sermons may have radically changed. Nevertheless, for what they may be worth these discourses are offered to my friends.

They were preached at the Riverside Church, New York, and, in slightly condensed form to meet time limits, over a national network of the American Broadcasting Company. To the loyal congregation that for twenty years has supported my ministry with a backing for which I can never be sufficiently grateful, and to the multitude of radio listeners whose encouraging response has made preaching seem profoundly worthwhile, my cordial thanks are quite inexpressible.

The absence of footnotes may prove troublesome to some readers, because I have freely used different translations of the Bible. The King James' version, the revised versions, Moffatt's translation, Goodspeed's, and Weymouth's have all been used. Each has its value, and if any reader is led by this volume to seek their acquaintance, he will, I am sure, find himself enriched.

To more people than I can name, especially to my secretaries, Mrs. Dorothy Noyes and Mrs. Rudolf Neuburger, I am deeply indebted. This volume is sent to the press after my retirement from the full time responsibilities of parish ministry and, reading it over, I feel sure that any one must perceive in it the accent of an older man, assuming the right to recall personal reminiscences and to share his experience with his younger contemporaries. Not only to those, therefore, who have aided me in preparing these sermons for publication but to those who may read them with considerate understanding and good will my cordial gratitude is due.

Harry Emerson Fosdick

August 1, 1946

Acknowledgments

THE author wishes to express his appreciation to the following publishers and agents for permission to quote from their copyrighted works:

Mrs. George Bambridge, Doubleday & Company, Inc., The Macmillan Company of Canada, Ltd., and A. P. Watt & Son, London for "The Explorer," by Rudyard Kipling, from *The Five Nations*.

Doubleday & Company, Inc. for "Prayer of a Soldier in France," from *Poems, Essays and Letters*, by Joyce Kilmer.

Harper & Brothers and Brandt and Brandt for the lines from *Renascence and Other Poems*, by Edna St. Vincent Millay.

J. B. Lippincott Company for *Watchers of the Sky*, by Alfred Noyes.

The Newspaper PM, Inc. for the lines from *Notes for Now,* by Bonaro Overstreet (April 16, 1944).

Charles Scribner's Sons for "The Marshes of Glynn" and "A Ballad of Trees and the Master," by Sidney Lanier, from *The Poems of Sidney Lanier*.

ON BEING FIT TO LIVE WITH

"It is easier to fight for our principles than it is to live up to them."

ALFRED ADLER

On Being Fit To Live With

"A YEAR of disenchantment . . . remarkable for the number and magnitude of illusions which have perished in it" —that fairly well describes this twelvemonth following World War II. Yes, but those words were written in 1867 after the war between the states. We are not the first generation to live through post-war disillusionment, with its confusion and dismay. The futility of war, the transiency of its victories, its fecundity in producing problems worse and more numerous than any that it solves, this is an ancient experience. What distinguishes our generation in dealing with it is the global scale on which it confronts us. Never before has the whole human race been involved together in such a general and inclusive catastrophe as ours.

Many, therefore, stand looking at the world's calamity as at a gigantic spectacle, its problems so staggering that we, as individuals, feel unrelated to it, our ability irrelevant to its solution. I do not see how we can stay there, however, if we perceive what the gist of the world's problem really is: being fit to live with. Our one world calls desperately for that. Wives and husbands, parents and children, Russia and the United States, Britain and India, Orientals and Occidentals, whites and Negroes, Roman Catholics, Jews and Protestants—the world, with catastrophe awaiting failure, is crying for those qualities of life and character that make men and nations fit to live with.

If this seems oversimplification I agree that it is a minimum statement, but it has this advantage: it presents a responsibility none can deny, each of us knowing that he is under obligation at least to be decent to live with, and each of us also day by day either adding to or subtracting from that basic quality—fitness

[1]

to live together—without which no problem in the world can ever be solved.

Paul was dealing with this matter when he wrote his twelfth chapter of First Corinthians: "Many members, but one body. And the eye cannot say to the hand, I have no need of thee: or again the head to the feet, I have no need of you . . . whether one member suffereth, all the members suffer with it; or one member is honored, all the members rejoice with it." Applied to our world's estate now, that simile represents a momentous fact: races and nations forced to live together, before we are fit to live with. Facing that kind of situation, Paul swung out into his thirteenth chapter on love, driven to it by the logic of the situation, seeing that only love can meet the issue. That is not simple, but penetrating, far-reaching and profound.

Of course, being fit to live with is the secret of a good home. Many associate broken homes primarily with outright infidelity, but any personal counselor sees homes where even adultery has been forgiven but where some other things can no longer be endured, and other homes too he sees where infidelity did not come first, but last, after a long, long series of other troubles had paved the way. It is what many people call little things that commonly break up homes—sullenness, moodiness, hypersensitiveness, irritability, petty jealousy, quarreling, nagging, bad temper—that is to say, the things that make folk unfit to live with. As one wife said about her husband who was an actor, "He was a comedian on the stage, but he was a tragedian at home."

Some of us came from homes lovely to live in, and considering what made them such we see why Paul moved out from his twelfth chapter into his thirteenth. That is what it takes to be fit to live with in a home: "Love suffereth long, and is kind; love envieth not; love vaunteth not itself, is not puffed up, doth not behave itself unseemly, seeketh not its own, is not provoked, taketh not account of evil . . . beareth all things, believeth all things, hopeth all things, endureth all things." Our theme is not oversimplification. It fathoms the depths of our lives; it is about the loveliest thing that can be true of us, that we are really fit to live with.

On a large scale, this is the world's problem. Today we all are thinking of the vast political overhead the United Nations is trying to build up—absolutely indispensable. But here in the church of Christ, consider the foundations of it all, the spiritual bases on which alone a peaceful world can stand. Races and nations decent to live with—that alone will do it, and one by one we individually are in the thick of that. Every unfair discrimination a white man practices against a Negro, every nasty slur voiced by a Gentile against Jews, or by a Jew against Gentiles, every expression of contempt against a whole race or nation, every outburst of meanness, discourtesy, prejudice and bad temper, makes less possible the solution of mankind's gigantic problem. Our theme brings the whole world's deepest need within the scope of every man's responsibility.

We have always talked about world brotherhood. It was a beautiful ideal, but now the entire aspect of the matter has altered, world brotherhood no longer an ideal but the absolute condition of civilization's survival. It is world brotherhood now, or else!

To be sure, for decades the realistic facts of world-wide interdependence have been creeping up on us, but still we have clung to old nationalistic ideas, picturing the world's peoples, to use another's metaphor, "as strung together without continuity, like wash on a line." But for a long time now the world's races and nations have been growing less and less like "wash on a line," their economic interdependence, for example, becoming more obvious every year. Where do our telephone instruments come from? Japanese silk, Indian mica, Malay rubber, Irish flax, Russian platinum, Egyptian cotton, South African gold—these are a few items in an ordinary telephone.

On Being Fit To Live With

This kind of thing, after a fashion, we have known, but now, the dramatic conquest of the air, the shrinking of the planet in travel time, and the release of atomic power, have suddenly confronted us with history's most momentous crisis, long building up but unmistakably here at last—races and nations forced to live together before we are fit to live with. The most serious aspect of this situation is that being fit to live with is a spiritual matter; it can be politically expressed, but it cannot be politically manufactured; it must start in the intelligence, conscience and good will of people. Can we meet that test of survival now? And it takes us all in!

We should be able to do this much: stop talking about international peace, world brotherhood and all that, as beautiful ideals. They are no longer ideals, but hardheaded, desperately necessary endeavors to catch up with the realistic facts. It is the facts, not the ideals, that have gone far, far ahead of us—facts of conquered distance, compulsory interdependence, enforced propinquity, inescapable relationships as members of one body—the facts have outdistanced us, and every endeavor after world brotherhood is simply the spirit of man trying to catch up with the facts before it is too late. As Prime Minister Attlee said, "We cannot make a heaven in our own country and leave a hell outside." No! The day has passed for that.

The phrase, "being up to date," is commonly used in trivial ways, but think what it means to be up to date now! At the very least, it means being citizens of one world. Josiah Quincy was one of the early legislators of this nation, but in 1811, when the admittance of Louisiana to the Union was proposed, and was violently resisted by the Federalists, Josiah Quincy said in Congress: "If this bill passes, the bonds of this Union are virtually dissolved . . . as it will be the right of all, so it will be the duty of some, to prepare definitely for a separation—amicably if they can, violently if they must." So lightly to propose secession from the Federal Union! How could he? He said once, "The first public love of my heart is the Commonwealth of Massachusetts.

[4]

There is my fireside; there are the tombs of my ancestors." See, we should like to say to him now, you were far behind the times when you talked like that; the welfare of Massachusetts was involved in the Union; it could never be well with Massachusetts without the Union; intelligently to care for Massachusetts meant putting the Union first; only with national loyalty and unity paramount could any state be safe.

It would be easy for us so to talk to Josiah Quincy, but we ourselves are in a similar case. Now for us to put the nation first is to be disloyal to the nation. The world comes first. It can never be well with the nation unless it is well with the world. If the world goes to hell the nation will go with it. To see that, to act on the basis of that, in personal and public attitudes to become citizens of the world—that is just catching up with the facts. More than that, it is catching up at last with the New Testament: "The field is the world."

We Americans had better watch our step now! We naturally take it for granted that we are fit to live with. Granted, we are doing some good work, but we are close to being the most powerful single nation on earth, and we had better not flourish that power around, as we are tempted to. What if some other nation—Russia, for example—were the most powerful on earth? What if she alone possessed the secret of the atomic bomb's manufacture? What if she in the Pacific blew up millions of dollars worth of ships with her bombs, and what if she frankly said what our American admiral in charge of the experiment has said is the purpose of it: first, to translate the result "into terms of U.S. sea power"; and second, to train "Army Air Forces personnel in attack with atomic bombs against ships." Suppose Russia were doing that, how would we feel?

Alas, all the great powers, Russia not least of all, now are trying to move in two directions at once: on one side supporting the United Nations to abolish war, and on the other beginning what may prove to be the most fatal competitive armament race in history to prepare for war—in this country proposing to establish, for the first time in our history, universal military conscription in peacetime. The nations cannot pursue both those purposes at once—not for long! May God bring all of us up to date before the bell tolls! As our own Secretary of State put it: "There must be one world for all of us or there will be no world for any of us." So, whether in a home or the world this is man's critical need—to be fit to live with—and it takes us all in.

Consider now that if we are to meet this momentous issue anywhere, in a home or a neighborhood or a world, we must follow Paul out from his twelfth chapter into his thirteenth. A Biblical scholar once whimsically said that one of the strongest arguments he knew for the inspiration of the Scriptures was that they had survived their division into chapters and verses. Nowhere has that division been more disadvantageous than in First Corinthians. Sometimes we read the twelfth chapter by itself, and forget what comes after; often we read the thirteenth chapter by itself, and forget what went before. But when Paul wrote his letter, what we call the twelfth chapter poured out like a river into the thirteenth; the moving current of his thought demanded it. If we are many members in one body, then hate will not do; vengeance, ill will, selfishness—not by them can the problems of such interdependence be solved; only love can solve them.

Love in the New Testament is not a sentimental and affectionate emotion as we so commonly interpret it. There are three words in Greek for love, three words that we have to translate by our one word, love. *Eros*—"erotic" comes from it—that is one. In vulgar use it meant sensual lust; in Platonic philosophy it meant the yearning of the soul for the realm of the gods. The New Testament never employs that word; both in vulgar and in philosophic usage it had connotations that would not do. *Philia*—that is another Greek word. It meant intimate personal affectionateness and friendship. The New Testament does use that, twenty-five times, when intimate affectionateness is meant.

[6]

But the great Christian word for love is something else: *agape*. Over two hundred and fifty times the New Testament uses it, and *agape* means nothing sentimental or primarily emotional at all; it means understanding, redeeming, creative good will.

The New Testament commands us to love, for example, but no one can command us to feel intimate affection for another; that is not within our volition's power. What the Christian God can and does command us to do, however, is to practice always and everywhere, with friend and enemy, with neighbors close at hand and with strangers we have never seen, an understanding and creative good will. "Whatsoever ye would that men should do unto you, even so do ye also unto them"—that is the expression of *agape*. "Love your neighbor as yourself"— that is *agape*. "Love your enemies"—it is nonsense to command that, if it means feeling affection for our foes; but if it means, as it does, extending even to them an understanding, saving, creative good will so that, by God's grace, enemies may at last be turned into friends, that makes sense. Love the Russians, millions of them, love the Chinese, the Indians, the South Sea Islanders, and all the rest—no wonder men think that idea silly when they interpret it to mean emotional affectionateness. But to extend to the Russians, the Chinese, and all the world, understanding and creative good will—that is not silly, but the *sine qua non* of civilization's survival now.

A little child in a family I know heard the phrase, "human beings," and asked its meaning. "It means all of us," was the answer, "father, mother, brother, sister, our neighbors. Everyone we know is a human being." "But," said the child, "all the people we do *not* know—are they human beings too?" That is the towering question now, and *agape* answers it. To see all men near and far as sons of God, to practice understanding and creative good will to all men as human beings—that is the Christian ethic.

Just now this is critically important because so many of us are relying on a lower range of motive. Fear, for example—

will not the atomic bomb frighten mankind into brotherhood and peace? Well, the atomic bomb presents an ominous alternative, and there can be a constructive use of fear, but no man or nation was ever yet frightened into real brotherhood and peace.

Along with fear, we are relying on selfish calculation to save us. We can have nothing, we say, that we do not share. Freedom from deadly epidemics is a world-wide matter now; we must share health with all men if we are securely to possess it ourselves. So we argue about one good after another, from economic welfare to freedom from the tragedy of war. That is all true! No major good can be possessed in this new world unless it is shared—we had better say that! But such selfish calculation by itself alone can never bring real brotherhood and peace.

When American missionaries went to the South Sea Islands did they argue it all out that some day there might be a world war, and American boys might come there, and so, on the basis of selfish calculation, Christ had better be preached and practiced there first? They did not! They never thought of it! It was the Christian gospel that took them there, stronger than fear, nobler than self-interest, all men children of God, all men the object of Christ's redeeming sacrifice, love the law of life, mankind one family with every soul priceless in the sight of God—that, and that alone, took them to the South Sea Islands, that alone transformed cannibals into folk finely fit to live with.

This recognition of the New Testament's meaning of *agape* dissolves the too strict lines of distinction, now currently drawn, between love and justice. To be sure, these two are not identical. All of love is not included in justice, but the deepest meanings of justice are included in love, and without love and the insight and understanding it confers justice inevitably degenerates into injustice. The Golden Rule, the essence of justice, is not outside, but within the boundaries of Christian love, and today it is the political implementation of the Golden Rule in some effective form of world government that most concerns us. Only so can we be fit to live together.

The political difficulties in the way everyone sees, but behind them are the emotional difficulties inside the hearts of men. Were there ever such sweeping mass emotions of distrust and suspicion, vindictiveness and hatred on earth before? In George Bernard Shaw's play *Major Barbara* is a character, whose conscience, so the quotation runs, is clear and her duty done, when she has called everybody names. Such people bedevil the world, and mankind's hope lies in those who resist such regimentation by vindictive mass emotions, rising above them to an altitude more far-sighted, constructive and redeeming.

How did Abraham Lincoln ever do that, as he did, during the Civil War? "With malice toward none, with charity for all," he said. He was not soft. He was the wisest man of his generation, and his wisdom consisted, how much! in his ability to rise above the popular passions of vindictiveness. "I have not suffered *by* the South," he said to a friend, "I have suffered *with* the South. Their pain has been my pain. Their loss has beeen my loss." In retrospect how high his character towers, how constructive his wise statesmanship! In our world now there are vicious evils to be ended, their resurgence made impossible, their guilty perpetrators punished. But God help us, for our children's sake, to rise into *agape* and in a redeeming peace, that at last will take all nations in, to do for the world what so-called justice, without *agape*, can never do!

Ah Christ, you are the answer still! We want world brotherhood; all that we and our children most desire depends on that, but neither fear nor calculating self-interest alone can achieve it. We must have faith—that is basic; we must have hope—that, certainly; and we must have love. And if we are to be really fit to live with, in families, neighborhoods, nations and one world, "the greatest of these is love."

Are We Part of the Problem or of the Answer?

EVERYWHERE today the word "problem" confronts us. Listening to the radio or reading the morning paper we face a jungle of huge and complicated difficulties involving all mankind, and in comparison our small lives appear impotent, no bulldozers to clear jungles with but feeling rather lucky if we have a fairly comfortable corner of the jungle to settle down in. Each of us is tempted so to feel, but there must be a healthier way than that to face this generation.

Suppose there were no problems in the world. God might have made this universe like Aladdin's palace, all complete for our lazy occupancy, no difficulty to face, nothing new to discover, nothing puzzling to solve, nothing required but to settle down and luxuriate. After even a few weeks of that, can you imagine anything more boring? Instead, God has introduced us into this wild, raw, unfinished world to bear a hand in its completion—which means that human life's very essence is facing problems, being waked up by their demands, and that only so has mankind's growth in intellect and character been possible. To be sure, I often want to tell God now that it is being overdone, with difficulties so huge they frighten rather than stimulate, but in wiser hours, even in a generation such as this, one feels the challenge and the stir, so that an older man like myself understands what that editor about to be beheaded in the French Revolution meant when he said, "It is too bad to take off my head. I wanted to see how all this is coming out." That, at least, is the starting point of a healthy attitude.

One cannot stop there, however. We as individuals, small though we are, are not outside the world like spectators on the bleachers watching a game. Willy-nilly, we are all in the thick of the world's game, participants in its winning or its loss, with this question rising for each of us: Am I myself part of the problem, or part of the answer?

We have a traffic problem on our American highways, for example, where millions of automobiles run, where death and worse than death, a dreadful toll of maimed and mutilated lives constitutes a cruel and needless sacrifice of health and happiness. Well, you drive an automobile—are you part of the problem or of the answer?

We have a family problem in this nation, broken homes a public menace, with moral standards cracking and marital infidelity a national disgrace, yet made a joke of in popular movies and best-selling novels. Well, are we part of the problem or of the answer?

Our theme ranges far this morning and goes deep, and here is a text for it. One full moonlight night in Palestine I stood on the summit of Mt. Tabor and, looking fifteen miles across the plain to the dim shadow of Mt. Gilboa, thought of the ancient days when Saul was King of Israel and when, perhaps on such a night, he slipped away from his army and sought the Witch of Endor in her cave, there on Little Hermon far below me. Note this: in the twenty-eighth chapter of First Samuel we read, "Now Saul had cleared the mediums and wizards out of the country." So, he recognized witchcraft as a public evil, and had issued an edict against it—all witches and wizards, begone! But four verses afterward we read this: "Saul said to his courtiers, 'Find me a witch, that I may go and consult her.'" That is one of the most human passages in the Bible—a man recognizing a public evil as evil, but when the pinch came becoming himself part of the problem. All witches begone! but four verses afterward, Seek me a witch!

We all behave like that. Nothing would be much easier than to stir this congregation with a moving sense of the evil of race prejudice. In our time have we not seen an exhibition of it so barbaric that it leaves us turbulent with indignation? In our own country who of us does not regard the Ku Klux Klan as a public menace and disgrace? But when all of us are thus unanimously stirred by recognition of this cruel public evil, let each of us turn inward to himself and see what secret racial antipathies he harbors, what primitive shrinking at the color line he feels, what irrational discrimination against some other race he practices. Even in so obvious a matter, are we part of the problem or of the answer?

In a deep sense no man can help being part of the world's problem. "All we like sheep have gone astray." "All have sinned, and fall short of the glory of God." There is no avoiding that. Do our best, we still are sinners, participant in the world's evil. Our modern thought has belittled sin, made game of it, called those who stress its dreadfulness puritanical, and has even laughed morality off as a mere changing fashion. That is cheap thinking. See what sin really is! In a world with difficulties enough already, with the fortunes of our children dependent on their solution, sin takes us one by one and makes us part of the problem. That is not a little matter, but treachery against mankind, and we are all involved in it.

Nevertheless, once in awhile we do see someone concerning whose character we feel, That is the answer! Given enough such quality, such spirit and behavior, and the world's problems could be solved. It is for that we plead today, and sinners though we are, by God's grace every one of us can in some degree attain to it—not so much part of the problem as of the solution.

Considering this theme, let us first face our powerful temptation to make exceptions of ourselves. Saul did that, and who doesn't? Witchcraft a public evil—he saw that. But when his own bad days closed in, the old superstition resurged in him and he made an exception of himself: "Find me a witch, that I may consult her."

In this congregation that kind of thing is surely going on. About the church, for example! You would not bring up your children, would you, in a community where there were no

Christian churches? You recognize that the church problem in this country is of deep public concern, and that to have the right kind of churches in our American communities, powerhouses of inspiration for private character and social service, is of first-rate importance. You see that the surrender of the churches to unintelligent leadership, their desertion by those who might have been expected to stand by them, and the consequent lapse of those faiths that produce character and that perpetuate the great spiritual heritage of our race, is a public peril. Almost everyone, of whatever religious background, grants that. Yet in New York City there are over a million Protestants unassociated with any church. Well, I am asking some of you, are you part of the problem or part of the answer?

One of the noblest statements of the moral law ever made was phrased by Immanuel Kant: "So act that thou canst will the principle of thine act to be law universal." That is to say, so live that if everybody acted on the same principle it would be well with the world. But, alas! seeing objectively the principles whose universal application would be well for the world, how commonly we subjectively make exceptions of ourselves! The black market a social peril, but we patronize it. Drunkenness a public menace, but we drink too much. Honesty basic to all business, but we try an undercover deal. Bad temper one of the most damning evils in a home, but we let ourselves be the terrible tempered Mr. Bang. The religious education of our children a national need, but with our children we let it slide. In one realm after another, All witches begone! but then, we say, Seek me a witch! Or as modern psychology puts it, we rationalize, with endless excuses dispensing ourselves from obligations that we wish all others would observe. Food should be sent to starving Europe, surely! but then when the chance is given us to help, we don't. That everybody should side-step responsibility for the church, Oh, no, not that! but then we do. Longfellow went to church once and wrote in his diary when he came home, "John Ware, of Cambridge, preached a good sermon." And then he added these five unusual words, "I applied it to myself." So may God grant this morning!

One reason why we thus throw off the sense of personal responsibility is that the public difficulties are so huge that what a man does with his own life seems of small account. No matter what he does, still like glaciers the world's affairs move on their relentless way. What does his life matter? That is a familiar defense mechanism now.

When I began my ministry over forty years ago the situation was reversed. Then it was difficult to get Christians interested in public problems, and we who believed in the social gospel had to shout to make ourselves heard. You there! we said, trying to save your own souls, come out of your absorption in your individual faith and salvation and see the application of Christian principles to the world at large! Now, however, in intelligent circles at least, times have changed. We are all interested in public problems—how can we help it? They are immense, spectacular, obsessing. Our own and our children's destiny depend on their outcome. We live and move and have our being in an atmosphere of anxious concern about huge problems.

So today the Christian minister finds himself changing his tune. You, so concerned about the world's situation, he says, it is downright hypocrisy in one area after another to cry aloud that we must cure mankind's evils when our own lives are part of the evil to be cured. This, at least, is a man's responsibility—to move his own life over so that he is part of the solution. And what a godsend a man is who does it, so that seeing him our hearts cry, That kind of living is the answer!

Let me speak for a moment especially to you young people, growing up in a generation when the idea of moral law as something objectively and eternally there—some things everlastingly right and some things everlastingly wrong—has so largely broken down, the great standards of right and wrong no longer recognized and morality made a matter of as you like it, of what you as an individual can find pleasure in, and can get away with. How prevalent that idea is everyone must see. The way I behave is my private business, a youth says. To which I answer, The way you behave is most certainly not your private business; it is the world's business. From this dilemma no man can escape: he is either part of the world's problem, or part of the answer, and that is not just your private business or mine. In this country now it is estimated that some four million people drink far, far too much, to the obvious hurt of themselves and all around them, and that hundreds of thousands of them are chronic alcoholics. That is a national menace, affecting the whole country's life. What an individual does, therefore, in that regard, is not his private affair alone. Am I part of the problem, or of the answer?

As a preacher I worry because so much of our preaching is like sheet lightning; it is general; it concerns the great evils of the world and the great ideals we should pursue. This morning I wanted to bring some forked lightning in that would hit something, as though one talked to the Prodigal Son in the Far Country and found him, as might well be the case, quite worked up about the world's moral evil and the ill consequence it resulted in, and as though one said to him, Son, you are right about the world's evil, but just now you are part of it. What about solving that much of the problem? What about your saying, I will arise and go unto my Father?

This leads us to the most positive and constructive aspect of our theme, namely, the inspiring effect of even one life that does that, concerning which we feel, That kind of living is the answer. A youth recently came to see me all down in the dumps because this is so vile and ugly a world. I said to him, "You are a youngster. You don't half know how vile and ugly the world is. Do you know, for example, that today there are ten million people in India totally blind, and thirty million more partially blind?" "Good heavens," he said, "I didn't know it was as bad as that!" "Well," I answered, "it is as bad as that. No youngster like you can half know how bad the world is. But listen! Those people do not need to be blind; the causes are all known—vitamin deficiencies and the rest. And a Christian missionary physician, Dr. Victor Rambo, has gone into India with the answer that in widening areas is redeeming, and if he is properly backed will redeem the Indian people from blindness. He says it can be done, and he is starting on it. Now which are you going to bet on, in the long run—the evil, or the solution, when already the solution is visibly at work?" Well, even that down-in-the-dumps youth could not resist the pressure that moved him over from being aghast at ten million blind people in India, to being excited by a person who incarnated the solution. That youth started by saying, How awful! He ended by saying, How marvelous, to be in a game like that!

Friends, that's life in this wild world—vast problems, and then someone comes, seeing whom, we cry, That's the answer!

Is not this one of the central meanings of Jesus to the world? Born in a manger, died on a cross, no wealth, no prestige, nothing to count on except those intangibles of character that cynics belittle, and yet across the centuries towering still, the life concerning whom more and more people know that he is the answer. Where his spirit comes, that is the solution, and just as in science, though all mankind thinks a disease incurable and only one man has found the remedy, a new era has dawned, so Christian faith is sure about Christ in the long run against all the world's evil. As one troubled soul said, "Son of Man, whenever I doubt of life, I think of Thee."

Today we are saying that each of us in his own degree can thus be part not of the problem but of the solution, and that kind of person is about the most inspiriting sight we see. I thank God for some I know. They keep me going.

To be sure, there are some people here who, I fear, may be hurt by this sermon. The burden of their life is that they do feel themselves part of the problem—economically dependent, ill, handicapped, mutilated, it may be, in the war, stopped in their tracks by physical disablement so that they feel themselves leaners, not lifters. To some such person here this sermon so far may have been like a stinging whip. I am part of the problem, he may be saying, part of the world's burden, and I cannot help it.

Friend, listen! Nothing in this world is more inspiriting than a soul up against crippling circumstance who carries it off with courage and faith and undefeated character—nothing! You too can be part of the solution. Mr. Newton Baker, Secretary of War in President Wilson's cabinet, told me that after World War I he used to visit in the Federal hospitals the worst casualties of the American Army. One of the very worst was a man with both legs gone, one arm gone, both eyes gone, his face terribly mutilated, who was wheeled around the grounds of the hospital in a perambulator by a nurse, but who still was radiant and full of spirit. Nobody expected him to live. When later Mr. Baker met somebody from the hospital he said, "Did that young man live?" And the answer was, "Did he live? I'll say he did! He married his nurse!" Marveling at the capacity of women to love, Mr. Baker put the matter by, until a few years later as trustee of Johns Hopkins University he received a letter from the president. They wished, said the president, to do an unusual thing, to hold a midsemester convocation to bestow the degree of Doctor of Philosophy upon a young man who, though heavily handicapped, had done one of the most brilliant pieces of work ever done at the University. His name was that of the crippled veteran. Mr. Baker, quite incredulous that it could be the same man, but struck with that phrase "heavily handicapped" made inquiries. Sure enough, it was he! Both legs gone, one arm gone, both eyes gone, but still, not part of the world's problem but part of the answer.

Not every handicapped person can win through to so conspicuous a result, but the spirit—the spirit that stays undefeated in spite of everything—is part of the solution, and those of us still strong and well who see it take another notch in our belts and go to our tasks again with fresh courage.

As for the moral and spiritual realm, what we have been talking about this morning is personal conversion—by God's grace to be so inwardly changed that a man passes over from being part of mankind's disease to being part of the cure. Whenever that happens it makes a difference to the whole race. No little thing that Prodigal did when he came home, not little for himself nor for his father, nor for the world. That event is still one of mankind's unforgettables. God grant that it may happen here today, for in the long run everything depends on enough people who are part of the answer.

Science Demands Religion

ABOUT one saying of Jesus' I never thought of preaching until recent events luridly lighted it up: "Except ye repent, ye shall all likewise perish." Today those words come not alone from Jesus but as well from a strange second to be singing a duet with him—modern science. Shattering the atom, in retrospect, may prove to be more important than all the rest of World War II, and its threatened consequence pairs up with Christ today—a strange, momentous combination—to say to us, Except ye repent, ye shall all perish.

The Master's saying was called out by two tragic events in his time. First, Pilate murdered some Galileans while they were sacrificing in the Temple; and second, the tower of Siloam collapsed and killed eighteen people. In both cases, apparently, popular sympathy was not with the victims but against them. Those Galileans, said the people, and those upon whom Siloam's tower fell, must have been especially wicked sinners or God would not have permitted such ruin to befall them. So ran the old-fashioned doctrine which great books like Job had long since been written to disprove, but which still hung on—that pre-eminent disaster always implies pre-eminent guilt; that when we see a great sufferer we see a great sinner. Jesus, however, was impatient with all that. He said:

> "Do you think, because they suffered this, that these Galileans were worse sinners than the rest of the Galileans?
>
> I tell you, no; unless you repent you will all perish as they did.
>
> Or those eighteen men killed by the fall of the tower at Siloam?—

do you think they were worse offenders than the
    rest of the residents in Jerusalem?
I tell you, no; unless you repent you will all perish
    as they did."

The voice which says that to us now is modern science, especially in view of the atomic bomb. We invented it; we used
it; we blotted out at a flash over a hundred thousand civilians,
men, women and children. When our self-justifications are all in,
every one of us is none the less horrified at the implications of
what we did. Saying that Japan was guilty and deserved it, gets
us nowhere. The mothers and babies of Hiroshima and Nagasaki
did not deserve it. Rather, before we are through thinking about
it we run straight into Jesus' words. Henceforth war means for
all of us just such ruthless, indiscriminate obliteration of civilian
populations. We ourselves have made war mean that, and the
crucial fact that faces mankind now is just what Jesus said it
was: "Except ye repent, ye shall all likewise perish."

Consider this strange thing that has come to pass. Science
has turned preacher. It mounts the pulpit. It says what some of
us in our wildest dreams never supposed we should hear science
saying. Look to yourselves, science cries to mankind; you had
better repent; those spiritual values, those inner secrets of life's
ethical control that can wisely master and direct the powers put
into your hands—these are necessities now. Hiroshima and
Nagasaki are but the first dim, tame intimations of what war
henceforth will mean. Except ye repent, ye likewise!

Our western world has faced four relationships between
science and religion. First, science was in bondage to religion;
no scientist dared contradict an established dogma of the church
but, imprisoned within the confines of ecclesiastical authority,
faced fearful penalties if he should transgress.

Then we passed into the second stage. Science broke free
from dogmatic bondage. Its pioneers won for science its rightful

liberty. At first, what this new liberated science did was shocking to the church. It broke down old world views on which as on a trellis the faith of millions had been entwined. It discredited one dogma after another, forced the radical reinterpretation of the Bible, and violated ancient sanctities of opinion with what seemed to many blasphemy, until the antagonism between science and religion was tense and bitter.

Then, for intelligent people, that second phase passed. Too many first-rate scientists remained good Christians, and too many good Christians welcomed all that science had to offer, for the idea to hold on longer that science was religion's enemy. But still, science was religion's competitor—that was the third phase. Both science and religion were ways of meeting human need. What chance had religion in that competition? One field after another science took over, supplying what men want and for which in vain they had prayed to the gods for ages. From scientific agriculture, engineering, and the invention of conveniences, to medicine and psychiatry—what need of man, without or within, would not science meet? So multitudes began to think, and in our generation one of the major obstacles Christianity has faced has been the growing popular feeling that religion is unnecessary and irrelevant, that what we most urgently want, science can supply. That is the third phase, and it has affected millions in our time.

Now, however, the door opens wide on the fourth phase. Science has put into our hands power that chills to the marrow-bone thoughtful folk around the world, power utterly to destroy ourselves and our civilization. As long as you young people live you will face the problems of this fourth phase. Science no longer in bondage to dogma—that is gone. Science no longer the enemy of religion—for intelligent Christians that is gone. Science no longer the competitor of religion—that is not the crucial matter now. Now a new era begins—science preaching like an evangelist, with hell and heaven on earth to choose between, saying to mankind, Seek wisdom and character that can control these powers for mankind's good! Repent of war, and of all that leads to it, lest you perish utterly! Seek world-wide good will, and faith too, that men are not merely brutes who must obliterate in utter ruin all that man has gained! I can give you power, says science, but by myself alone I cannot guarantee what will be done with it. Something more than myself must decide that, something that mankind has always called its religion, - the spiritual values it ultimately cherishes, the faith about life's meaning it supremely holds. In God's name, says science to religion, if you still believe in God take him seriously, and somehow get control of what I am giving you,—or else ye shall all perish!

This is far too great a matter to compass adequately this morning, but note briefly its relevance to certain aspects of our lives.

For one thing, it should come home to us personally. My generation has lived through the most amazing scientific age in history. Yet now as we face the world the great scientists have produced, all that they have done is not enough—even for one personal life in its depths.

> Science is my shepherd; I shall not want.
> It maketh me to lie down in green pastures;
> It leadeth me beside still waters.
> It restoreth my soul:
> It guideth me in the paths of righteousness
> for its name's sake.
> Yea, though I walk through the valley of the
> shadow of death,
> I will fear no evil; for science is with me;
> Its rod and its staff, they comfort me.

No! No one can say that. That is not enough!
The fact rather is that because of man's misuse of scientific gifts we older people have had to live through the most colossal

breakdown of optimism in history. You younger people who have come to social consciousness since 1918 cannot possibly imagine the mood of optimism in which we were reared. We lived in the days of the first telephones, the first express trains, the first uses of electricity, the first internal combustion engines, the first of so many ingenious devices that we stood on tiptoe wondering what new marvel would appear tomorrow. We were the natural disciples of Herbert Spencer and his gospel of inevitable progress. Were I to talk today as nineteenth century optimism talked, you would think me an arrant sentimentalist. And the reason is that the high hopes built on these scientific achievements, which we welcomed with such acclaim, have crashed to the ground as man has proved to be so insane, so corrupt, that the more power you give him the more he will destroy himself. And now the flash of the atomic bomb lights all that up with frightening clarity.

Let us take this to ourselves personally! Do we, for example, one by one, find New York City an easy place to handle well, ethically and spiritually? Everything that science gives the individual is here, but alas! each of us needs something greater than science gives—deeper, more inward, spiritually sustaining, controlling and directing life; and we need that the more urgently the more science gives. I wish that for a moment I could abdicate this pulpit and that you could see here, not a Christian preacher, but science standing, with all the gifts it so munificently bestows, saying just what Jesus said: "A man's life consisteth not in the abundance of the things which he possesseth." Indeed, it doesn't! A man's life consisteth in his inner rectitude of character, his basic faith about life's meaning, his inner resources of spiritual power to control life and direct it to good ends. Science itself is saying that today, as I never dreamed it would.

Note further now that this truth should come home to us not only as individuals but as citizens. Who of us ever expected to hear a President of the United States say what President Truman said the other day: "We can't stand another global war. We can't ever have another war unless it is total war, and that means the end of our civilization as we have known it."

Popular reactions to the atomic bomb have been diverse, but the most futile of them, I think, is the wishful thinking that supposes we can now outlaw atomic power and go on having war without it. That is an escapist's dream. Throughout war's history humanitarians have always been shocked by the latest weapons and have insisted that they be outlawed. Martin Luther justified war as necessary, but gunpowder—that ought not to be used, he thought. What Luther said about gunpowder and the guns that use it reminds one of what many now are saying about the atomic bomb: "Cannons and fire-arms are cruel and damnable machines, I believe them to have been the direct suggestion of the devil. Against the flying ball no valor avails; the soldier is dead, ere he sees the means of his destruction. If Adam had seen in a vision the horrible instruments his children were to invent, he would have died of grief."

So humanitarians have always protested against each new weapon, while all the time war has gone grimly on, developing and using them just the same. When the machine gun was employed by Kitchener to mow down the charging hordes of the Mad Mullah in the Sudan, British humanitarians were horrified. War, yes; but not machine guns! In that kind of vain hope many today are still trusting. The destructive core in each of those two bombs dropped on Hiroshima and Nagasaki was hardly larger than an apple, and yet four of those apples, we are told, equaled in explosive power all the bombs sent against England in the whole course of World War II. To suppose that with such power available it will not be used in any future war, is fantastic.

To be sure, atomic power brings with it promise as well as peril. Hopefulness is always present in any problem that centers in the handling of power. I have been in places on this earth, among the tribes of the Sinaitic peninsula and of Trans-Jordania where not power but weakness was the problem. Penury, the edge of starvation the habitual habitat of the people, no science, nor any power that science confers—there was little hope in that. Then one turns to our western world. It is ominous. I am not taking back a single thing I have said about our situation. Yet not weakness is the matter with us, but power, and that is hopeful, if—God help us to fulfill that if!—if we achieve the character, the faith, the spiritual quality, to master the use of that power for mankind's good.

A leading scientist in this nation, speaking to a friend of mine the other day, pulled an ordinary cardboard railroad ticket from his pocket and said, "There is enough atomic energy in that to run an express train ten thousand miles." And then he added, "We'll tackle sand next. Sand! And in two handfuls of sand there is energy enough to supply all the basic power needs of the United States for two or three years."

Imagination boggles and breaks down, trying to grasp what has happened to us. But this central matter is clear: the towering question before mankind today is not physical power—we have more than enough of that in sight—but spiritual power to handle it. I never expected to live to see science frightened at its own discoveries of power. But listen to the scientists! They are frightened. They have cracked open the illimitable arsenal of solar energy, and mankind must handle it. The signals of distress are up in every scientific mind I know. S.O.S.! Ethical control wanted—a spiritual life and faith adequate to master and direct to saving ends the might our hands have seized upon! "Except ye repent, . . ."—it is the scientists now who most clearly see the alternatives to that! It is not a preacher but Einstein who says: "In the light of new knowledge, a world authority and an eventual world state are not just *desirable* in the name of brotherhood, they are *necessary* for survival—otherwise we face certain disaster."

If to us personally and as citizens this truth is relevant, it surely is to us as Christians. I have been saying that science demands religion, but it is not any kind of religion that science demands—it is great religion. No other kind will do any good in this emergency. Plenty of religion merely litters up the premises. Our sectarianism, our conventional Christianity, has no relevance to the vast, crucial problems of our time. But when one steps into the Gospels and listens to Christ speaking: "Seek ye first the kingdom of God, and his righteousness"; "Whatsoever ye would that men should do unto you, even so do ye also unto them"; "He that is greatest among you shall be your servant"; "Thou shalt love the Lord thy God with all thy heart, and with all thy soul, and with all thy mind. This is the great and first commandment. And a second like unto it is this, Thou shalt love thy neighbor as thyself"; "All they that take the sword shall perish with the sword"; "Blessed are the peacemakers: for they shall be called the children of God"; is there any doubt that such religion is precisely what our sick world needs? In that sense, it is Christ or chaos now; Christ, or mankind's suicide.

In the underground physical laboratories in Columbia University one day in 1941—it may have been, for all I know, a Sunday morning when we were at worship here—one of the preliminary experiments that led to the fission of the atom came to a successful issue. It was a nervous hour; they were not sure just what would happen; perhaps everything would blow up. Ever since I heard about it that scene has haunted me. Across the street, a few hundred yards away, the most momentous discovery of physical power in all history getting started, and we here preaching Christ. Once, a casual onlooker, skeptical of religion, might have viewed that contrasting scene with condescension and, it may be, with contempt toward our Christian worship. There in that physical laboratory the big business was afoot; but we, with our Christ, were escapists, were we not? trying to find comfort for our own souls in an imaginary world of ideals and hopes. Now, however, I do not see how even a skeptical onlooker can be content with such an attitude. What came out of that physical laboratory demands ethical control. Unless we are all to perish—ethical control! By itself that discovery is not the biggest business. The biggest business is the spiritual power to use it now that it is here.

It is going to be a long hard haul. It will require patience, courage, faith that hangs on when hope fades, if we are to tame the rude barbarity of man so that the atomic age becomes blessing and not curse. It is going to take us all, and all there is in us. Don't stay on the side lines! No one of us has any business on the side lines. Take hold somewhere—as persons, as citizens, as Christians—on behalf of that great religion of faith and character, without whose incorporation in a new world order and without whose mastery of our new and awful powers we shall indeed all perish.

On Getting Christianity Out of Its Pigeonholes

SOMETIME since, an important symposium was published, summing up the major areas of our generation's life: its arts and sciences, its industry, education, politics and recreation. There was no chapter on religion, and when the editor's attention was called to the fact he said, "Well, no one of us thought he knew enough about religion to write about that." That editor's picture of the modern world is clear—a secular civilization spreading around the globe, with religion in general and Christianity in particular, not only playing no dominant part in it, but off in a pigeonhole where folk like himself need not even bother to think about it.

Even a secularist may well be disturbed by that picture now. How do we like it—a world where man's profound concerns with God and the soul and the eternal moral law are put aside in pigeonholes, to which indeed some turn for private help and comfort, while mankind's vast affairs move on as though those pigeonholes did not exist? As Professor Montague of Columbia University puts it: "For perhaps the first time in history we are confronted with the prospect of a complete secularization of the opinions, the practices, and the emotions of mankind."

Today we shall not talk to the secularists about this for they probably are not here, but to ourselves as Christians, because the fault is largely ours that Christianity has been thus relegated to pigeonholes. It is we who need that totally different idea of Christ's meaning, which the New Testament presents. Says the Book of Revelation: "The kingdoms of this world are become the kingdoms of our Lord, and of his Christ." So! No cubbyhole his realm; no segregated, sacred compartment of life the object of his conquest; but as Dr. Goodspeed translates it, "The sovereignty of the world has passed into the possession of our

[28]

Lord and his Christ." Business and politics, national life and international relationships—he came to take possession, not of a fenced yard called religion, but of all mankind's day-by-day ordinary life.

This is Layman's Sunday, and the truth we are dealing with carries Christianity's major meaning straight out into the layman's realm. We say Christ came to save individual souls. Yes, but that is not all. We say he founded the church to be the nucleus of his faith and ethics. Yes, but that is not all. Christ, seen as the private possession only of individual souls, or of the church, is segregated in a compartment of life, and there he may stay while the affairs of the world go on, secularized, dominated by a pagan faith and ethic that land us where we are today. It is not on what happens here in church on Sunday that Christ's eyes are ultimately set, but on what happens to-morrow, out in the world where you laymen move. Do we really believe that, or have we, too, with all our worship of him, really put Christ into a pigeonhole?

For one thing, we make him Lord of a niche in life by dividing life into the sacred and the secular. How familiar an attitude that is—most of life secular; we do not think of God with reference to it, and to think of Christ dominant in it would be positively embarrassing. To be sure, Joseph Jefferson did say about his fellow actor, Edwin Booth, that behind the scenes he ran his theater as though it were a church, and once when a cowardly clergyman who feared his congregation's disapproval wrote Booth, asking whether there were not a back door in his theater where he could slip in unobserved, Booth wrote back, "There is no door in my theater through which God cannot see." The popular view, however, sees most of human life in secular terms, but with a sacred niche in it where we do think of God, and perhaps pray, and recognize at times our dependence on a power greater than our own. Many have accepted that popular outlook on life.

The falsity of this partition of life—a vast secular world with a sacred niche in it—becomes clear as soon as we seriously ask the question, Is Christ's truth really true or not? I am not thinking now of the complicated theologies that have grown up about him, but of his own central affirmations: that we are all children of one God; that brotherhood is the basic law of life; that human personality is of infinite value; that God's world is a world of moral law where injustice and tyranny and selfish greed and racial prejudice are everlastingly wrong, and where no lie can last forever; and that the eternal purpose proposes here on earth a kingdom of righteousness. You see, if such basic affirmations of Christ are true anywhere, they are true everywhere, not in any sacred pigeonhole only, but in business and politics, in national life and international relationships.

Some things can be put in a corner. Collecting stamps, reading detective stories, playing golf—they belong in life's pigeonholes. But some things essentially belong to the whole of life, and Christ's faith and ethic are one of them. When Einstein states a cosmic law the world faces an issue: is it true or not? If it is true, then it is universally true and not in any niche in life alone. That the world faces that kind of issue about Christ today is shouted from the housetops by the ghastly situation the world confronts. We have secularized our modern world; we have conducted the mass of its affairs on pagan principles. Are they true? Does it look as though they were true? Or is Christ's basic ethic in solid earnest the revelation of the everlasting moral law, that men and nations violate at their peril? Then, being thus true, it is true everywhere and about everything, and we had better get it out of the pigeonholes where we have put it.

There are many ways of getting rid of Christ—theologically denying him in philosophic arguments, or practically denying him, saying, like Hitler, that his ethic is only for cowards and weaklings—but in Christendom the most popular way of getting rid of Christ is to split life into two realms, the secular and the sacred, and then put Christ away in a sacred niche within whose confines we treat him with great respect. Think of him there today, pigeonholed, and we must see that he is struggling to get out. He dealt with ordinary life; his words are all colored by it and concerned with it; he was no ecclesiastic; all life was his concern and the whole world his care. He is crying for help, and his call comes especially to you laymen. Get me out of this sacred niche where you Christians have put me, he says; my truth was meant for business and politics, and racial relationships, and national and international life; I did not die to save a pigeonhole, but the whole world.

Face now the fact that in this cornering of Christ in a sacred compartment of life the sectarian churches have had a guilty share. We Christians pity Jews who through the cruelty of their oppressors are compelled to live in ghettos, but there is, as it were, an ecclesiastical ghetto into which we Christians have put Christ. When from the large affairs of the world, on which the destiny of men and nations depends, one goes into this ecclesiastical ghetto one hears such questions as this: Are we Methodists, or Presbyterians, or Episcopalians? How much water was used when we were baptized? Do we believe in this or that ancient miracle story? Do we think this or that theory of apostolic succession is necessary to constitute the true church? Believe it or not, a leading Protestant paper in this country recently said that anyone who eats his breakfast before partaking of the *Lord's Supper is guilty of gross sin, comparable with fornication. So we Christians have built an ecclesiastical ghetto into which we have put Christ. Read the Gospels and see the kind of person he really was! Can you imagine him happy, cooped up like this? I suspect the Crucifixion itself was not harder for him to bear than this segregation of his universal truth within the petty sectarianisms, the theological quibblings, and the ceremonial routines of the ecclesiastical ghetto.

Do not misunderstand me! I think the church may yet be

the saving leaven in the lump. One of the most hopeful things in the world today are powerful movements in the church that are getting Christ out of these pigeonholes. Archbishop Temple of Canterbury, for example, was an Anglican, with the natural loyalties of an Anglican, but when he thought of Christ he thought, not first of Anglicanism, but of the world. Here we are, he says, with ever greater and greater aggregations of political power, armed with ever mightier implements of inventive science, and between these vast aggregations of power ever stronger tensions dividing them. Something must be put on top of all this unless we are to be destroyed. And that something cannot be merely a super-state, important as world organization is; it must be the moral law, of justice, decency and humaneness, recognized as the everlasting truth about life, to whose sovereignty men and nations owe allegiance, and will give it, or else perish. Such is the church's real message now, not for a sectarian cubbyhole, but for the world.

The other day I was introduced to one of our leading actresses who said that for many years she had wanted to thank me for a service once rendered her, that had been a turning point in her life and had enabled her to gain and keep a vital religion. Years ago, she said, I picked up by chance a magazine article of yours in which you said, "God is not a Baptist." That is all she remembered of the article. To be sure, she said, I was not troubled about the Baptists because I had never been one, but my God was all cooped up in the sectarian ecclesiasticism of the communion I had been trained in; I could not believe in that God any more; and your phrase opened the door, and my God got out into the world. If putting the matter as simply as that can help, I wish that might happen here today. Of course God is not a Baptist, or any other kind of ecclesiastical sectarian! Do we not believe in monotheism yet —one universal God, not only Father of all mankind, but the rightful sovereign whose moral law is everlastingly true, for every department of man's life?

This truth carries the major meaning of God and his Christ

straight out into the realms where you laymen live. The church's critical need today is laymen and laywomen who believe that Christ's truth alone can set us free, and who therefore are determined that the convictions and principles he stands for shall in the end be worked out in all our public life. Ah, church of Christ, you had better wake up to that vision! Recently in one of our communities the church building burned down and two neighbors found themselves standing side by side, watching the blaze. Said one, "This is the first time I ever saw you at church." Said the other, "This is the first time I ever saw the church on fire." Well, the church of Christ had better be on fire today!

Note now another way in which we segregate Christ in a sacred niche: namely, by a wrong use of intimate personal religion. One of the commonest ideas today is that religion is a private affair, between a man's own soul and God, a perpendicular relationship that links the individual to a divine source of help, which is nobody's business but his own.

You will not understand me to deny the truth in that. I preach it continually. Personal Christianity is a profound inward relationship between the soul and God, and its innermost expression, as Jesus said, comes in solitiude in a chamber with the door shut. If someone says that that inner relationship with the divine is the very root of Christian experience, I agree. But that is just what it is—the root, the invisible, underground, vital root; but it is not the fruit; and any Christianity that tries to be all root is just as much a failure as a tree would be that tried the same impossibility.

In particular, during these ghastly days of strain much of this secluded, pigeonholed, private religion never gets within range of the idea that Christ needs the whole world to operate in, and that the whole world needs Christ. From the radio audience comes a letter which says: "We so-called atheists are or seem to be very brazen most of the time, but I am coming to the conclusion that we are just 'whistling in the dark,' and when the crisis comes we find we are not quite sufficient unto ourselves and call on a God in whom we profess not to believe, for aid and for comfort and for help." So even supposed atheists in a crisis turn to this inner, secret, sacred niche in their souls and seek help.

If ever anyone emphasized and valued this inner companionship with God, Jesus did. Whenever he saw it he rejoiced, calling it vital leaven. But listen to him: "The kingdom of heaven is like unto leaven, which a woman took, and hid in three measures of meal, till it was all leavened." So Jesus was thinking, not primarily of the precious leaven but of the whole mass in which it was placed, the entire world, its industry, its politics, its education, its racial and international relationships —there lay his ultimate concern, till it was all leavened. As Paul put it, "A little leaven leaveneth the whole lump."

I am talking now to someone here who enjoyed what we said in criticism of the churches. Such talk was bowling down your alley. You have never had much to do with the churches anyway, and to hear a minister go for them was entirely agreeable to you, for your religion has been a strictly private affair between your own soul and God, and nobody's business but your own. Well, our truth is on your trail now! You, too, are putting Christ in a pigeonhole and a mighty small one at that—your own private experience. Believe me, he wants to expand beyond that cubbyhole! Tie yourself and all you know of Christ in with the organized fellowship that at least is trying to apply his principles to the world's affairs. Come over and help us as a layman in the church to make it an instrument for mankind's help. Turning one corner of your own soul into a religious retreat and supposing that to be the whole of Christianity is to misunderstand it utterly.

The gist of the matter is that Christianity is not merely a sacred, ecclesiastical or private affair, and so, as is commonly supposed, the minister's specialty. Beware of that idea that the minister is a specialist in Christianity, who is supposed to take care of it! All the ministers together, no matter how good they are, cannot take care of Christianity; that is not their business. Their business is to help create laymen and lay-women who out in the so-called secular world where Christianity faces paganism—dreadful paganism, so that all we hold most dear is at stake—will take care of Christianity until the whole lump is leavened.

None of us wants the church, as church, to control education, politics, national life and international relationships. As a professor of economics in the University of Lyon, France, once put it: "It is not the function of the Christian Church to create a new civilization; it is the church's function to create the creators of a new civilization." I should think you would want to be one of them if only for the sake of your own children. You build a lovely home, a segregated, sacred place, where you teach your children high ideals; you send them to a church school where they are taught the faith and principles of Christ; and then they go out into that other world—politics, economics, total war—and see what happens to your children! It is not homes, schools and churches that in the long run most educate our sons and daughters, but that world out there in which they are compelled to live. Lincoln said this nation could not endure half slave, half free. Surely this world cannot endure half sacred, half secular; it is bound to be more and more either one or the other.

When Handel's *Messiah* first was sung in London two hundred years ago, an unpremeditated, spontaneous response led first the King and then the whole audience to rise and stand during the Hallelujah Chorus, and we still do that now. It is not the music only, but the central faith the words enshrine, that calls for that, and it is all about the layman's realm: "The kingdoms of this world are become the kingdoms of our Lord and of his Christ . . . King of Kings and Lord of Lords. Hallelujah!"

What The Law Cannot Do

IN THE eighth chapter of Paul's letter to the Romans a familiar verse begins with an arresting phrase: "What the law could not do." The limitations of law, the things that legal regulation cannot accomplish—that should be worth considering in a generation like ours, so tempted to trust laws and more laws, government and more government, to save the world.

Now Paul honored law. As a Jew, the moral law laid down in Scripture had his full devotion, and as a Roman citizen he was proud to live under the most majestic structure of civil law the world had known. Both the Roman and the Jew in Paul honored law, but all the more impressive is his insight into its limitations: "What the law could not do, in that it was weak through the flesh, God, sending his own Son in the likeness of sinful flesh and for sin, condemned sin in the flesh: that the ordinance of the law might be fulfilled in us, who walk not after the flesh, but after the Spirit." Phrased thus in terms that to modern ears may sound archaic Paul's meaning none the less is clear: two things set in contrast—the prescriptions, coercions and penalties of a legal system on one side, and on the other the creative power of the spirit revealed through Christ, which produces new quality of life inside people. Concerning this contrast Paul is saying what our modern world urgently needs to hear, that when men trust legal regulation to do what only creative spiritual life can do, they are riding for a fall.

Every society has these two aspects: on one side, its regulative, coercive laws; on the other, its spiritual culture. The one works through politics, departments of state, bureaus of governmental administration and courts of law; the other works through homes, schools, churches, the fine arts, personal religion. The one organizes and regulates life from without; the other creates life from within. An old story runs that Napoleon Bonaparte, informed that under his regime there had been a decay of French letters, and that there was need for a renaissance of creative literature in France, answered, "So! I will speak to the Minister of the Interior about it." But that divine afflatus, that wind of the spirit blowing where it listeth, from which great literature comes, no department of state can produce. There are things law cannot do.

For obvious reasons our generation is absorbed in governmental problems, extending the scope and tightening the control of law. Mankind's major problem now is the building of world government, with international law implemented and enforced; and within the nation the growth of immense aggregations of power, whether gigantic industrial corporations on one side or labor unions on the other, compels the extension of government's control to protect the interests of all the people. Let none misinterpret this sermon as belittling the tremendous importance of regulative and coercive law. But it is in just such a situation when we are thinking, and ought to think, of what law can do, that Paul's emphasis on what law cannot do becomes the more cogent.

In the long run the law can get out of the people no more goodness than there is inside the people. The law is much like a pump, and the water it pumps is the intellectual, moral and spiritual life of the people—no better, no worse.

Once in this country we had a prohibitory law concerning alcoholic liquors, constructed with all the precision of legality and backed by a Constitutional amendment, but when it started working, what did it pump? Just what was inside the people, no more, no less. However hard we worked the pump, it drew only what was in the people. In a generation trusting government for salvation, as few generations have ever done, we had better remember that.

In these critical days our prayers are with the United Nations, our hopes are centered there. What the law can do, God grant it may do now! But here in the church of Christ, representing that other aspect of society, its inner creative moral and spiritual life, we face the sober fact that even the United Nations, like a pump, can draw no more good will, good sense, mutual understanding and unselfish devotion to mankind's welfare, than exist in the hearts of the world's people. All the organs of publicity will be talking now about world government and the way to make it work, but who will speak about that more inward matter, the moral and spiritual life of the people, which government may extract but cannot create? For when these great pumps we now are building start to work, we shall again confront the fact that they can draw only such moral and spiritual life as is in people—no more, no less.

We Americans say that the Constitution made our nation. The Constitution is a magnificent document, but it took more than that to make the nation. Rather it was our forefathers and foremothers who made the Constitution, and then made it work. The government they constructed got great things out of them, but it was not the government primarily that put the great things into them. What put the great things into them was their home life, their religion, their sense of personal responsibility to Almighty God, their devotion to education despite all difficulties, their love of liberty and their personal character. When their government pumped, it drew from profound depths in lives where creative spiritual forces had been at work.

This is an old lesson in history that we critically need now. In 388 A.D., before a full session of the Roman Senate, Theodosius, the Emperor, put the question whether the worship of Jupiter or the worship of Christ should henceforth be the religion of the Romans, and Christ won the day by a large majority. So the Roman government became Christian in 388. But alas! that did not make Europe Christian. If the world could be saved by law, how often its salvation would have come! No! Everything we want most in the world depends upon those deeper levels of life for which Christ stands, where not coercive and regulative law but creative spirit must work the transformation inside the lives of men. Now is the time, not to forget but to remember that.

Come further now and see that this brings us all into the picture. What can we do, folks say, in this tremendous era? But it is we who are the gist of the matter. Woodrow Wilson said once, "Our civilization cannot survive materially unless it be redeemed spiritually." Surely it is not the law's function to do that. What redeems men spiritually is deep and inward, individual and personal; it works through homes, schools, churches; it comes in the still small voice of conscience; it is the message of Christ's gospel to men's souls; its consummation is man's welcome to God's spirit so that life is personally transformed. Our civilization cannot survive materially without that, said Woodrow Wilson; he would certainly say it now.

We of this generation stand on the verge of an era that may see the death of our civilization. I am not thinking alone of the atomic bomb, although the end may come by that dramatic instrument, but, behind that, a civilization always dies first of all at the roots; it dies in the spirits of men; it dies in the death of the forces that make men creative and loyal and right and strong within. Professor Collingwood of Oxford, speaking of our own times, writes: "Civilizations die as they are born, not with waving of flags or the noise of machine guns in the streets, but in the dark, in a stillness, when no one is aware of it. It never gets in the papers. Long afterward a few people, looking back, begin to see that it has happened." Sometimes in the stillness of the night, thinking of what is going on in the world now, I wonder if that is happening to us.

If our civilization is not thus to die, it will take more than law to save it. It will take a profound moral and spiritual revival. In the eighteenth century the English-speaking world faced a desperate situation. Never, I think, had Christianity reached a much lower ebb than then. Crime increased, morals collapsed, licentiousness was rampant. So the people, as always, turned to government to save them. They tightened the rigor of the law and compounded the penalties—the number of crimes punishable by death was appalling—but it was not that which solved the problem. What solved the problem was an amazing revival of spiritual life in general, and of religion in particular. We call it the Wesleyan movement, but it was far deeper than any technical religion, and far ampler than could find deposit in any church. It broke up the fountains of the great deep in the British and American people; it brought in a new day in literature as well as in the churches. Lord Shaftesbury and his industrial reforms cannot be explained without it. Wilberforce and the ending of the slave trade were the children of it. What the law could not do, God did in men who walked after the Spirit.

Here I am, supposed to be a modernist, preaching up a revival! You know well that I mean nothing superficial, emotional only, merely ecclesiastical. I am thinking of what the most serious minds of our generation are thinking. Chancellor Hutchins of the University of Chicago is no preacher and would not wish to be called one, but he is saying that the material side of our civilization has so far outdistanced the moral and spiritual competence of our people to handle it that the outcome now depends on whether our moral life can catch up, and can catch up quickly enough, to save the day. That takes us all in, saying to each of us, What about your life? Are you part of the moral and spiritual renewal by which alone civilization can be redeemed?

Come at this from another angle and see that with all our rightful devotion to government and its laws, we must make use of other agencies also if we are to save the world, namely, the voluntary agencies that spring from the spirit of the people.

One of the most colossal problems confronting mankind is the relationship between Russia and the United States; we are all worried about it, and everyone is looking to the United Nations to solve it. What the United Nations can do is desperately important, its wise handling of affairs indispensable, if catastrophe is to be escaped. But given a few years—as may God grant!—in which to work this relationship out, there are things the law cannot do that voluntary agencies must undertake. You scientists! get in touch with Russian scientists and establish fraternal relationships with them. You educators! team up with Russian educators and share your experience and skill. You church of Christ! get as close as you can to the Russian Orthodox church and go as far as you can in establishing fellowship. All wise observers in Russia bear witness that if their common people could know our common people, and we know them, there could be understanding and mutual respect, and that the last thing any of us want is war. Oh, I know, there is that "iron curtain" now, but in this modern world that cannot last long, and in the meantime it will take more than government to get around it; voluntary agencies must outflank it, people seep through it, and establish relationships with the Russian people. Ultimate peace with Russia may in large measure depend on things the law cannot do.

The church of Christ especially has a supreme opportunity. She can go where laws do not reach. With her humanitarian service, her medical missions, her friendly lives going for love's sake where no one else would go, she can do what no political set-up can get at at all. Look at what Christian missions have done in China,—one of the most saving factors in that distracted land—and see what the church can accomplish that the law could never have done! Stand by her! She needs you! She is at work on the spirits of men, on the intimacies of character and human relationships, without which, no matter what governments decide, the epitaph of our generation will be at last: "What the law could not do."

You businessmen in your realm feel the force of this thing I am trying to say about the limitations of law. You do not like totalitarian government that thinks it can do everything, and you are disturbed as statism crowds out free enterprise. To be sure, you must grant that the motive of private profit, gone haywire, can do dreadful things, and that modern technology is creating wide areas where, for the protection of the public, the state's power must be extended. But you are right about this substantial matter: it is not law alone that makes the clock tick in any realm. Law can regulate, coerce, control, but it does not create. Law can set the scene that makes creation possible and can maintain conditions that stimulate and encourage the creative life, but still living things grow from their own deep roots, and creativity comes from inward motives, faiths, loyalties, hopes. All the law in the world could not have produced Beethoven, or Einstein, or Edison. Handel, fifty-six years old, poor, his right side and his right arm paralyzed, writing the Hallelujah Chorus because he saw the heavens opened and heard the angels sing—you cannot get anything like that in any realm by law. Creativity lies beyond law's scope, and it is creativity, initiative, moral enterprise we want.

The pioneers who made this country were not under law. As Kipling said,

> ". . . a voice, as bad as Conscience, rang interminable
>   changes
> On one everlasting Whisper day and night
>   repeated—so:
> 'Something hidden. Go and find it. Go and look
>   behind the Ranges—
> 'Something lost behind the Ranges. Lost and waiting
>   for you. Go!' "

So they ventured into unknown lands and carved great states out of the wilderness, driven by an inward call to their courage and their faith. To be sure, it took law to civilize the frontier, but we Americans do not want to lose that other element of personal initiative out of this country and we are right.

That is what I am driving at in my special realm today. Spiritual creativity is inward and personal, something that God does in men inspired by his Spirit, and the call to that comes home to each of us. What about it in your life and mine? If our civilization dies, it will die for lack of creative moral and spiritual life and that need must be met, not by legal coercion but by personal decision, by lives inspired from within to do what no law can ever command.

We come now to the most intimate application of our truth, that brings us closest to the thought of Paul. When Paul used the word "law," the majestic structure of the Roman legal code could not altogether have been absent from his mind, but most of all he was thinking not of that but of the moral law, laid down in the sacred Scriptures of his people, and he was facing the disturbing fact that moral law lays upon men obligations which it does not provide power to fulfill. It tells us what we ought to do, but it does not supply the strength to do it. "I delight in the law of God after the inward man: but I see a different law in my members, warring against the law of my mind, and bringing me into captivity under the law of sin which is in my members." Who does not face that experience—moral law commanding righteousness which it cannot provide power to fulfill.

A moving letter was written recently by a son in the South Pacific to his father at home. His father had been a drunkard. He knew the moral law, but had no strength to fulfill it. Then he came into touch with God and found a Power that did what the law could not do. His son came home for a visit after his father's amazing transformation had been wrought, and returning to the Pacific, wrote this to him:

"When I look back at how you've changed, Pop, it seems like something from a fairy tale. All fellows think that they have the best father in the whole world. You've always been the best father to me but now there's something else. I'm so proud of you, Pop, for what you've done in the past few years that it's better than being Lincoln's son or even Uncle Sam's. They did wonderful things for other people, too, but you've climbed the biggest barrier in humanity. You've conquered yourself. It takes a thousand men's wills and a million men's patiences to do that completely. I started to tell you how I felt when I was home but I never got through the first sentence. I'll still never be able to put into words how much I love you for what you've done for Mom, me and the kids."

That kind of experience millions of saved souls have known, and still the need of it is deep and critical. The law that says, You ought, without the power that says, You can, is frightening and futile. May some one here join the triumphant ranks of those who understand the secret: What the law could not do, God sending his Son can do, in those who walk after the Spirit.

What Does It Really Mean To Be Great?

AT NO point is Jesus more revolutionary than in his ideas about what it means to be great. His saying, "He that is greatest among you shall be your servant," is so familiar that its radical contradiction of agelong ideas of what greatness means commonly escapes us. Today, therefore, we start our thought, not with Jesus' familiar words, but with someone who never heard of Jesus, who lived centuries before him outside his race and nation, a representative of ideas of greatness that have dominated history. In the second Book of Kings we read, "Now Naaman, captain of the host of the king of Syria, was a great man . . . but."

What follows that "but" is serious: "but he was a leper." Across his greatness a shadow fell that turned it into tragedy, and so familiar a situation is there symbolized that already your minds are leaping far beyond the ancient detail of Naaman's special malady, for which he was not responsible, to feel the impact of a truth that men and nations critically need to face today and for which they are responsible: "Naaman was a great man . . . but."

One can imagine God saying to our era now: You are a great generation; you have achieved such scientific mastery of cosmic powers as your fathers never dreamed; you have spread the privileges of education to a degree that only a century ago would have seemed incredible; your standard of living has risen beyond all historic precedent; you have extended the average life span in this country until it is now about sixty-five years; your inventive skill has been so magical that today no spot on the planet is more than forty flying hours from the nearest airport; you are a great generation—but! What follows that "but" is ominous, ghastly, as anyone can see. Our idea of greatness does need

[45]

a revolution, and concerning it Jesus has a message on which our salvation depends.

Someone here, to be sure, may be thinking, This theme indeed applies to the world's large affairs, but it lets me personally out. I have no claim on greatness, or conceit concerning it. I see what the preacher means: Napoleon was a great ruler—but; Edgar Allan Poe was a great poet, but, alas! he died in a drunken brawl in a Baltimore saloon; Hitler was a powerful Fuehrer—but; many an outstanding historic personality is described by the text: Naaman—a great man, but! I am not one of them, however; my name will never be heard of outside the circle of my friends.

One who so is thinking may not, however, thus escape our theme's inclusive range. In every normal person is the desire, within limitations however small, to be somebody, get somewhere, amount to something. Greatness is relative; we seek it in varying scales; but none of us wants to be a nobody. As for our sons and daughters, we pray that they may get somewhere and do something in the world, not necessarily prominent but certainly worth while. The temptation to misunderstand greatness, therefore, to interpret success in cheap and shallow terms. assails us all, and what in the large we see in the world's Naamans, we see in the small in ourselves and our homes. The saddest day in many a family's life comes when they say about some son of theirs, He was a great boy—but.

We turn then to Jesus' proposals concerning greatness, predisposed, I hope, to listen to him, because both we ourselves and our world so desperately need a revolution in our ideas of what it means.

For one thing, Jesus obviously thought that no one could be great who was not humble. A radical contradiction that, of the idea of greatness that has dominated history! To be sure, humility is commonly caricatured as weak subservience, and to understand its meaning one had better not look in the dictionary for its synonyms, but for its antonyms—arrogance, pride, haughtiness, conceit, presumption, insolence, disdain. We understand humility best when we see its opposites, for in thoughtful hours we know that that proud Pharisee in Jesus' parable, thanking God that he was not as other men are, was not great.

Humility is commonly conceived as a gracious virtue that decorates to good effect the finer sort of lovely characters. It is more than that, however. Germany was a great nation—but! Here is the "but," in a quotation from Alfred Rosenberg, the Nazi philosopher: "A new peace shall make Germany mistress of the globe, a peace not hanging on the palm fronds of pacifist womenfolk, but established by the victorious sword of a master race that takes over the world in the service of a higher civilization." Does not pride go before destruction and a haughty spirit before a fall?

We had better take a fresh look at the Master's idea of greatness. Humility—so that as Paul says, we do not think of ourselves more highly than we ought to think; teachableness—that knows we need to learn; penitence—aware of the beam in our own eye before we seek the mote in a brother's eye; graciousness —that does not push arrogantly up into the chief seats at the feast, as Jesus said; humility is not simply a lovely, decorative virtue of sweet characters. For the lack of it the great empires of the world have fallen, and the dictators have licked the dust.

I have been preaching Christ for many years, but in these days he gains new meaning. He is so right, so unexpectedly, incredibly right! Even when his insight most shocks our realistic common sense, he turns out to be right.

So far as humility in personal character is concerned, we have indeed come over pretty much to his point of view. We do not admire insolence, arrogance and pride. Listen to this commentary, for example, on Sir Isaac Newton from a fellow scientist:

"The modesty of Sir Isaac Newton, in reference to his great discoveries, was not founded on any indifference to the fame which they conferred, or upon any erroneous judgment of their importance to science. The whole of his life proves, that he knew his place as a philosopher, and was determined to assert and vindicate his rights. His modesty arose from the depth and extent of his knowledge, which showed him what a small portion of nature he had been able to examine, and how much remained to be explored in the same field in which he had himself labored. In the magnitude of the comparison he recognized his own littleness; and a short time before his death he uttered this memorable sentiment: 'I do not know what I may appear to the world, but to myself I seem to have been only like a boy playing on the seashore, and diverting myself in now and then finding a smoother pebble or a prettier shell than ordinary, whilst the great ocean of truth lay all undiscovered before me.'"

Newton was really a great mind.

More than personal significance, however, is in this truth. It applies to nations. Now that victory has come, what will it do to us Americans as a people? We are a powerful nation, we shall feel, and that will be true; but if that should lead us into proud, self-contained isolationism, or into proud, aggressive imperialism, or into proud, reactionary self-content, how really great would we then be? To many, it seems sheer sentimentality to apply to nations Jesus' beatitude, "Blessed are the meek: for they shall inherit the earth"—but is it? The teachable, who can learn from total war how necessary a world organized for peace is, the humble, who do not proudly separate themselves from the common weal or claim to be a master race, but recognize with modest wisdom that the welfare of each, however strong, involves the welfare of all—only such peoples have the slightest chance of inheriting the earth. From the days of Nebuchadnezzar, saying, "Is not this great Babylon, which I have built for the royal dwelling-place, by the might of my power and

for the glory of my majesty?" when have the arrogant, in the
long run, ever inherited the earth? All that

> ". . . . . . . pomp of yesterday
> Is one with Nineveh and Tyre!"

Today, with victory in our hands, I, for one, feel, not like shouting about my country, but like praying for her. God forbid that
our posterity, facing another total war, should ever have to say:
America was a great nation—but!

Another element in Jesus' idea of greatness was humane usefulness. "Whosoever would be first among you, shall be servant
of all"—that is one of the most revolutionary things ever said.
Observe that Jesus wants us to be great. He admired energy,
enthusiasm, competence. He had no use for lazy, listless, negative folk, and in his parables he took efficient, energetic businessmen, farmers, housewives and stewards as his examples. Far
from denying this powerful drive in human nature to be somebody, he counted it one of man's most valuable possessions, but
he raised a new criterion by which to judge what it means to be
somebody: serve most, help most! Usefulness—that is greatness,
he said. Never treat that as a platitude, for no more radical idea
ever emerged in man's ethical and social history.
Though we try to be cynical about it, saying that to be rich,
famous, possessed of power we can use for ourselves is to be
great, in our better hours we know that he is right. Once at
Saranac, in the Adirondacks, a withered wisp of a man, ill with
tuberculosis, was carried to his bed by a porter who said, "Why,
doctor, you don't weigh no more than a dried lamb-skin!" So
Dr. Trudeau made his entrance to the Adirondacks and there,
an exile, his own ambitions wrecked, began a ministry of healing
for countless folk who found life and hope because he was the
servant of all. Can anyone here, contemplating that, avoid an
inner hush of the spirit and a reverent salutation to a great life?
Some years ago a poll was taken in France to determine who

was popularly regarded as the greatest Frenchman who ever lived. Who do you think it was? No, not Napoleon! Pasteur, father of modern medicine, who sank himself in service! Despite all our contradictory ideas of what success is, if any man would be first, he shall be servant of all!

Indeed, at this point we face one of the miracles of history, that Jesus himself should be thought of as first. Why should that be? When he was born Augustus Caesar ruled the world, and when he died Tiberius was Emperor, and they were great. But he—a nobody, from a carpenter's shop in Nazareth, who never possessed power or station, unheralded by his contemporary world, hated by the powers that be, and dying on a cross—about him, nearly two thousand years afterwards, millions feel, as Charles Lamb felt, that if Shakespeare should come into the room we would all stand, but if Christ should enter, we would kneel. Yet all he ever did was help—that's all—no other greatness his, save this, that coming not to be ministered unto but to minister, he has been the servant and Savior of us all. Hardheaded, realistic world, scoffing often at what you call sentimental idealism, you are up against a law of life here, to which all history in the end bears witness: greatness—all greatness that lasts—is usefulness.

The personal message for each of us involved in this is clear: in this sense, we too can be great, every one of us, however humbly endowed or circumstanced. Somewhere, in some realm, each of us can share the only greatness that outlasts the fall of empires, and the successes that moth and rust corrupt and thieves break through and steal. We can help. As for our country, if a century from now our posterity, looking back, thinks of America today as great, you know they will be thinking, not so much how powerful and wealthy she was, endowed with what vast resources and what dominant strength, but this other simple, yet magnificent thing—she helped; in the most stupendous crisis of all history, when the world stood at the crossroads, with either total war ahead for our children or a planet organized for peace, America helped. This is the ultimate test of every personality, every economic system, every social custom, every political order—is it useful to the lowliest and the least?—and lacking that, all substitute splendor cannot prevent the final judgment: Naaman was a great man . . . but.

Still another element in Jesus' idea of greatness is, in some ways, strangest of all—obedience. In Gethsemane, bowed by sorrow and apprehension, something happened in him that made his emergence to face the cross one of the great events in history, and obedience was at the heart of it: Not my will, thine, be done. Jesus was a free, fearless, independent soul, but there was for him in this universe a Greater than himself, to whom he owed allegiance and whose will he obeyed. Without that, no real greatness!

You have been thinking this morning of some folk you know, concerning whom the fateful words hold true: a great man—but. We are not speaking now of little matters—frailties, faults and flaws of temperament, from which we all suffer and which our forgiving friends must pardon. No matter how nearly right we are, there is always a "but." Take that for granted! Not of small flaws that afflict us all, are we thinking now, but of those tragic failures that cast their shadows across all life; and what we are trying to say is, that nothing men call greatness can ever make up for lack of character, genuine character, obedient to the moral laws of God.

Psychiatrists tell us how half-witted boys, inferior and feeling it, get hold of powerful automobiles and driving them hard gain an illusion of greatness, importance and strength that are not really their own. Our whole civilization seems to be doing that, seizing on mechanical power and in controlling it feeling that it is great, when all the time it is as true of civilization as of a half-witted boy, that that is fake greatness; it cannot last; it leads to ruin. There is no substitute man's cleverness can find or his ingenuity invent, for character, obedient to the eternal moral laws.

If someone protests, I hate the idea of obedience, I want to be my own man, independent and free, I answer, God grant you may be independent and free! Bow your neck to no earthly subservience! But never forget that from one thing no man can be free—the eternal laws of living. Physical and moral, those laws were here first; there is no outwitting them. I know one man now, brilliantly endowed, eminent in his profession, greeted by the applause of multitudes—but! Behind the scenes he is using his brilliant ability as a substitute for character. He thinks he can get away with it, but already friends see tragedy creeping up on him; only a little further down that road the reckoning waits: Naaman was a great man . . . but!

Surely I am talking now to someone here about a real problem. Far from pleading for negative, unambitious, subservient living, we are pleading for greatness. The times demand it; the desire for it is in us all. At that point, however, the very devil enters, he too urging us to be great, but with meanings that ruin both men and nations. The proud Pharisee, thanking God he was not as other men, thought he had greatness, but we know now that in his arrogance he missed it. The rich young ruler thought he had it, but now we see that in his selfishness he never reached it. Pilate was sure he had it, Procurator of Judea and representative of Rome, but lacking character his epitaph is now like Naaman's.

Well, Naaman was cured of his leprosy, and Christ's gospel involves that for us. I want something important to happen here this morning in some lives, for our own sakes, for America's sake, and for the world's. Christ is everlastingly right about what real greatness means, and to the end of time all substitutes will come to that fateful conclusion, from which may God preserve us: Naaman a great man—but!

Take What You Want and Pay for It

A SPANISH proverb runs, "'Take what you want,' says God, 'take it and pay for it.'" That proverb does not cover the whole of life; some of our experience is beyond the scope of our choice; we have to take it, whether we choose or not. But at the center of life there is an area of personal selection where we pick and choose between alternatives, and where God does say to each of us, "Take what you want, take it and pay for it."

This commercial figure does not at first suggest Jesus' gospel of God's free grace and forgiveness, but Jesus, again and again, put life into commercial figures, and taught that everything we choose has to be paid for. The Kingdom of God, he said, is like a "pearl of great price," which a merchant, finding, "sold all that he had, and bought it." If you choose the highest, says Jesus, you must pay for it; or if you choose the worst, lawlessness, the judge, says Jesus, will "deliver thee to the officer, and thou be cast into prison. Verily I say unto thee, Thou shalt by no means come out thence, till thou have paid the last farthing." So Christ himself confronts us with the fact that whether one chooses the best or the worst, one pays for it.

Hitler chooses to be Hitler, and he pays the price; Niemoeller chooses to withstand Hitler, and he pays for that. Toscanini chooses to be Toscanini, and in self-dedication and self-discipline, he pays for it; and some debauchee selects, instead, a loose, libidinous life, and he pays for that. Let us look into this matter, for it goes deep, confronting us with facts we profoundly need to face.

For one thing, consider the lopsidedness of our ordinary thought of self-denial. When a preacher talks about the sacrificial

[53]

life it is commonly understood to mean one thing only, the cost-liness of goodness, the self-abnegation required in a clean, con-trolled, high-minded, useful person. Did not Christ say, "If any man would come after me, let him deny himself, and take up his cross, and follow me"? Surely, we agree, the kind of life for which Christ stands costs heavily. That is self-sacrifice, we think, to choose the highest and pay its price.

That, however, is a one-sided view of sacrificial living. Every-thing we choose, whether good or bad, we pay for. If a man chooses lechery and dissipation we commonly call it self-indulgence, but think again! Self-indulgence—to live a wasted, dissipated life? Upon the contrary, such living is self-sacrifice, the costliest self-sacrifice a man can make, giving up everything that most renders life worth while, throwing diamonds on the counter to buy dust.

Surely George Washington lived a sacrificial life, but so did Benedict Arnold, heaven have mercy on him! God said to both of them, Take what you want; take it and pay for it! Surely Christ lived a sacrificial life, but so did Judas Iscariot, poor fel-low!—with one of the greatest chances a man ever had, giving it all up for thirty pieces of silver and a rotting memory.

Some lives here could be profoundly changed by the recogni-tion of this fact, that we have to live a sacrificial life; there is no getting out of it; we either pay dust for diamonds, or diamonds for dust, one or the other. To some youth here I wish this might come home. Stop being fooled by the idea that you can choose between self-indulgence and self-sacrifice. That is a mere trick of words. All we can really choose between is two kinds of self-sacrifice. Take what you want, the good or the evil, take it and pay for it.

I thank God now in my elder years that I did not make some sacrifices when I was young. I had to choose, as all you young people must, which should be my aim, a Christian home with its deep fidelities and satisfactions on one side, or on the other, a loose life of sensuality. Well, I chose! Long before I met the

girl I married I wrote her a letter, in which I said that somewhere on earth I knew she was alive and waiting for me and
that some day we would meet, and that in the meantime I was
going to keep my fidelity to her as true as though she now were
mine. You say that cost. Of course it cost! But now in retrospect,
think what it would have cost had I made the other choice, to
have surrendered all the deep and sacred satisfactions of these
lovely years for a mess of pottage!

This is what our fathers meant by their old saying that "the
Devil is an ass." Indeed he is! Wicked? That does not half cover
it; he is an ass! He gets men to be Judas Iscariots and Benedict
Arnolds, telling them not to sacrifice but to indulge themselves.
He persuades the Esaus of the world to sell their birthright for
a mess of pottage. A clever ass the Devil is, but crazy too—as
though it were self-sacrifice to give up the low for the high, but
not self-sacrifice to give up the high for the low.

The gist of this matter is, of course, the fact that this is a
universe of moral law, no more to be outwitted than is physical
law. Look at our world and see! Twice in one generation mankind has chosen war, and God has been saying, As you will;
take it, and pay for it! From that to some personal decision
hanging in the balance here, this law confronts us. Pause before
you choose, my friend! Either way you are in for sacrifice.
Which will you give up for which?

Moreover, note this strange fact, that commonly when we
choose evil we get what we want at once and then pay for it
afterward; but when we choose good we have to pay for it first
before we get it. Why the world was made like that I do not
know, but so it is. The youth in college who chooses an idle,
lazy life can have that at once; today he can start that; he will
pay for it afterward. But the youth who wants a degree with
honor cannot get that today. He must pay for it before he gets
it, in hard work and self-discipline.

What a world! If a man wants a life of sensual excess he can

have that tonight, with all the wild thrill and mad sense of liberation that he seeks. He can seize his passionate desire at once,
and pay for it, it may be, long afterward. But a man who wants
a Christian character that, like a well-rooted tree, holds its own
against the storms of life and in the autumn bears fruit for his
generation's help, cannot get that at once; he must pay for it
first, and then get it.

Evil has this situation all set up in its favor. The cheap, the
low, the dishonest, the debauched choices we can have the gains
of quickly, what we want swiftly thrust into our hands. Take
it, the Devil says; never mind about the bills, they will come in
sometime, afterward. But the great choices, the long-term aims
that mean high character, high intelligence, great service—the
bills for all that come in first. In advance you pay for that with
devotion, concentration, self-discipline.

Kreisler vacillated for years before he made up his mind to be
a musician. As a small boy he began playing the violin, but with
such lack of success as discouraged him, so that he tried medicine, painting, military life, in a vain endeavor to find content-
ment there. Then he came back to his first love, decided that
come what might he would be a violinist and, making up his
mind to that, he started with eight solid weeks devoted to finger
exercises, and ever since has practiced the stern discipline that
alone can make a great musician possible. But now he is
Kreisler. For what he wanted, he had to pay first.

The results of this situation are, of course, deplorable. Mark
Twain's Huckleberry Finn summed it up. "Well then," said
Huckleberry, "what's the use you learning to do right, when it's
troublesome to do right and ain't no trouble to do wrong?" That
idea, shared by multitudes, comes largely from the fact that to do
wrong costs nothing in advance; we get what we want at once;
paying for it comes afterward. But to do right means paying in
advance—decision, discipline, devotion, loyalty.

I am talking to some youth here. Don't let this situation fool
you! Evil may be sold you on the installment plan, but believe

me! the bills at last come in. Huckleberry Finn is terribly mistaken when he thinks "it ain't no trouble to do wrong." It is—plenty—in the end, when the bills begin coming in! And the worst of it is that when the bills do begin coming in for your wrongdoing, they are not all presented to you; those who love you have to pay; those whom you do not really want to hurt, they have to pay. In God's name, don't run up bills like that, that years and years of paying by your family cannot satisfy! This, as much as any era in history, is a time for greatness. Choose the great goals, the long-term aims, high character, high vocation. Accept the fact that you must pay in advance, in self-control, self-dedication, self-discipline, for such superior goods. They are worth it. When the matter is at last presented to the arbitrament of retrospect, and from your elder years you look back upon your choice, you will know that it was worth it.

Come at this matter now from another angle, and see that hidden in this truth lies the reason for some of our most unintentional, and yet most deplorable hypocrisies. It is easy to choose the good in general, and then to fail utterly in paying the price of getting it. For Kreisler to say, in general, I want to be an artist, is one thing; it is something else to be willing, day by day, to pay the cost.

The nations of the world now are presenting a fearful illustration of this truth. Have we not chosen peace? Is not that what we want? If anyone should ask for war, would he not be howled down in indignation? It is peace we want, all are saying. But the price of peace—the necessary surrenders of national sovereignty, the cessation of power politics, the ending of competitive armament, the shift of our economy from self-centered nationalism to co-operative internationalism, the overcoming of racial prejudice, the building of a real world government where such suspicious remnants of the old order as the veto power in the Security Council have been overpassed—these conditions of peace, that must be fulfilled as indispensably as in a laboratory the conditions of achievement must be met, we shrink from. Give us peace! we say; but not the cost of it.

This is our peril now—a huge self-deception, concealed by the idea that we have chosen peace, as though a man said, I'm off for Bombay, and then got on a ship that does not go to Bombay at all. Once in Europe there were two contending kings, Charles V and his cousin Francis I. Charles V summed up the matter with admirable candor. "My cousin and I," he said, "are in complete agreement: we both want Milan." That is our trouble now. We say we want peace, but from oil in Iran to exclusive possession of Pacific islands, from the retention of subject colonies to the sole possession of atomic power, what we really are in complete agreement about is that we all want Milan.

Do not understand me to be discouraged. The road to peace is bound to be a long hard haul. But the nations desperately need to confront the realistic fact that peace is a good that must be paid for in advance. Look at the price of war! Can peace cost anything comparable with war's cost, that we should shrink from paying it? So let all the people cry, until our governments not only say that we want peace, but prepare to pay the price.

Jesus himself, applying this truth to personal life, put it into a hardheaded commercial simile: "For which of you, desiring to build a tower, doth not first sit down and count the cost, whether he have wherewith to complete it?" Who of us can escape that question? It is easy to make idealistic choices about towers—Christian homes, faithful marriages, the religious training of our children, integrity of character, public usefulness. Asked, in general, would we not say, Such are our choices? But the cost, have we sat down and counted that? Are we paying the price for what we say we want? What good does it do to choose the end and then not choose the means that alone can reach it? Many a family, knowing well this spring that it cannot have even a good garden without fulfilling the conditions, is still fooling itself that it can have a Christian home without sitting down and counting the cost. Our favorite hypocrisy is to make a lovely choice and then decline to pay for it!

To be sure, some here must be feeling that to their personal problem what we are saying is irrelevant, for something has happened to them which they did not choose, a calamity falling on them like fate, unwanted and lamentable—illness, bereavement, betrayal, poverty, crippling handicap. To them, the proverb with which we started seems cruel irony. "Take what you want, says God." No! they cry, life makes you take what you do not want!

Nevertheless, my friend, the power of choice is still yours. How will you handle it? What will you make of it? You can choose! You can be embittered, crushed, faith all knocked out of you and cynicism withering your soul. There, too, God says, If that is your attitude, take it, and pay for it! But you can choose another attitude. The most stimulating lives we know have suffered the bludgeoning of fate but still have chosen an unconquered faith, an undefeated spirit. As Emerson said, like the wounded oyster, they have mended their broken shells with pearl. That attitude costs too—deep faith, deep resources, great courage—but how inspiring it is to all who see! In God's name, take that attitude, and pay for it!

Nevertheless, our sermon needs an epilogue. Someone here must already have been thinking of it. We do not pay for everything. We get some things free. The great heritage of our race, the homes we came from, the gospel of God's grace in Christ, great books, great music, great art, great personalities—see this vast realm of benedictions we inherit "without money and without price." We do not pay for everything—that's true—but it has all been paid for.

As this Lenten season moves on, with the cross of Christ standing at its vista's end, that fact confronts us: free gifts life does bestow on us, but they have all been paid for. Here in our Church School, in a class of fourteen-year-olds, the question rose one Lenten Sunday why Christ had to die, and one of the boys volunteered an answer. "Jesus," he said, "saw a lot of good in this world, and he didn't like the way it was being pushed around. Somebody had to take the rap, and he took it." No theologian can improve much on that. That boy's homely speech, even, was like the New Testament's in using a colloquial figure to describe Christ's sacrifice. We have made elaborate theology of the New Testament's figures of speech about the cross, but at first they were as little conventional theology as that boy's description. The New Testament writers, thinking of Christ's sacrifice, went into the marketplace for their simile and said that Christ had bought us for a price. They went into the slave mart and said that Christ had paid a ransom for our liberation. They went into the law court and said that Christ had borne the penalty which we deserved. They went into the temple where, whether Jews or Gentiles, they were used to animal sacrifice and said that it was Christ's blood, his sacrifice of life, that saved us. We have made theology of all that, stiff, stereotyped, abstract, often incredible; but at first it was as real, as vital, as close to daily life as that boy's figure made it: "Somebody had to take the rap, and he took it."

Indeed he did! His cross represents a colossal fact that should make every decent man and woman pause. Free gifts are ours; all the background of our lives is full of them; but they have all been paid for. So here too we can choose—ungratefully taking all this free grace for granted, and, unappropriated, passing it up, *that* we can choose; or else,

"Lord, Thou didst suffer more for me
Than all the hosts of land and sea.
So let me render back again
This millionth of Thy gift. Amen."

The Urgency of Ethical
as Well as Economic Reconversion

GOVERNMENT and industry are busy now reconverting wartime into peacetime economy. War puts everything askew in business and finance, and the necessity of economic reconversion everybody sees. Yes, but to reconvert our morals and emotions also, to change them from a wartime to a peacetime basis—that too is indispensable.

Whatever else war makes abnormal it certainly has that effect on ethics. Millions of nice kindly people, who love little children and would not hurt one for the world, consenting to the obliterative bombing of whole cities, the mass slaughter of thousands of women and children at a single stroke—that is a sample of what war does to our ethics. If someone says that in war admirable virtues also shine out, I cordially agree. Coming back from France during the first World War, I remember saying that never again would I despair of human nature. I had seen such courage and fortitude, such self-sacrifice, such fidelity of men to their comrades and such willingness to die for a cause, that far from being depressed about mankind the thought of what such qualities harnessed to constructive uses could do in the world, was thrilling. But alas! in war, these noblest qualities of man are harnessed to the most frightful tasks man's imagination can devise. War's tragedy is that it uses man's best to do man's worst. What ethical chaos that anomaly produces—to use man's best to do man's worst! We are likely to get back to a peacetime economy long before we get back to a decent peacetime ethic.

At this point, some may be saying to themselves, The preacher is going to plead for kindness, good will, forgiveness, for mercy, sweetness, and light; he is going to soften us up if he can.

Plenty of people in this world could stand softening up! Kindness, good will, forgiveness and mercy are going to be desperately needed before this world is fit for decent folk to live in. But to say that first is, I suspect, not the way to get at our problem.

As Dr. Moffatt translates him, Paul wrote in his second letter to the Corinthians: "I do live in the flesh, but I do not make war as the flesh does; the weapons of my warfare are not weapons of the flesh, but divinely strong to demolish fortresses —I demolish theories and any rampart thrown up to resist the knowledge of God, I take every project prisoner to make it obey Christ." Living in a world of war, Paul considered himself a warrior too; only, he had an arsenal of spiritual arms. He fought against theories, ideologies, false and godless ways of thinking. He was engaged in ethical conflict. That passage certainly describes our business now. Once more a great war is over, and save as starvation and disease slay millions still, the killing has stopped, and what we face now is an ethical struggle. What an ominously difficult conflict it is going to be! Not softness then, but militancy of the spirit, armed with ideas, principles, faiths, and transforming qualities of life, is called for now. On that kind of ethical reconversion, from physical to spiritual conflict, the world's hope depends.

For one thing, war always means a progressive deterioration of moral standards. In January, 1940, Winston Churchill called the obliterative bombing of cities, "A new and odious form of warfare." That was Britain instinctively trying to cling to some ethical standard at least, even in wartime. But the obliterative bombing of cities went on and on, and in September, 1943, Winston Churchill said: "There are no lengths of violence to which we will not go." That is war! Every monstrous thing done by one side becomes excuse and justification for the same or a worse thing done by the other.

After every great war, therefore, comes a moral slump. The

standards have been broken down. What is right? What is wrong? Look at the things we have done in this war and called them right! No wonder letters come in from the armed forces like one that recently reached me. Is there any difference between right and wrong? the writer asked. Isn't it just a matter of fashion, of "as you like it," of what convenience or necessity dictates, of what you can get away with in this beastly world? Are there any ethical standards left?

The Christian response to that is not softness, but spiritual militancy going out into this generation to stand for the truth that God's eternal moral laws have not been cancelled and that there is no hope for us save as we establish an ethical gold standard.

I just quoted one soldier whose moral criteria were being shot to pieces. Here is another soldier, making a different response, a sergeant writing from a hospital in England where he has seen some of the children from the bombed cities:

"Seeing a soldier suffer is not so bad. . . . But kids, that is different. They didn't know what it was all about, just dazed, shocked and scared. It was no sight for me. Still, it didn't fill me with hate. It did make me realize that this deal can't be repeated again twenty years from now. We can't have our son, or anybody else's son, walking through a hospital looking at human derelicts; or worse, lying there having someone walk through and look at him. There is something wrong with the system, somewhere. I don't know if the cure is religion, or science or what, but this can't go on."

Young man, I should say to him, you are all set for genuine ethical reconversion. You are not soft; your fighting spirit is still up about war and what it does to people. This awful catastrophe has not broken your ethical standards down, but with a conviction you never felt before, you know that some things are eternally wrong, and some things eternally right.

[63]

We had all better take a fresh grip on that! Nothing can ever make Judas Iscariot right. Nothing can ever make infidelity, treachery, cruelty, hypocrisy, debauchery, right. Nothing can ever make war, and what it does to people, right. The standards have not collapsed—not even in special realms, like scientific research, where accuracy and veracity are everlastingly right, and not in ordinary life either, where decency, fidelity, loyalty and unselfishness are standards forever. Obscured though they may be, like mountains in the clouds, the eternal truths of the Hebrew prophets and of the Sermon on the Mount are still here; the great integrities call for our allegiance as never before in history. Only those who see that can help in ethical reconversion.

This at once becomes a personal affair. Economic reconversion is mainly a matter of large scale governmental and industrial arrangement, but ethical reconversion is intimate, private, individual. It all depends on enough persons who, one by one, deep within themselves, come through this world catastrophe with their central faiths and standards intact. What we are saying, then, gets down to a personal appeal. This coming decade, after the most awful war in history, is going to be ethically chaotic. Let's not fool ourselves about that, it is bound to be ethically chaotic, with the appeal coming to each of us, Don't be one more liability, your ethical standards all shot to pieces and your life going on the loose! Come help us in our reconversion to decency, and honesty, integrity and good will again!

Alike the difficulty and the necessity of ethical reconversion spring from another fact, that in war our trust is put preeminently in physical force, in the "weapons of the flesh," as Paul said, rather than in the persuasions of the spirit. For years mankind has looked for victory and deliverance to battleships, machine guns, flame throwers, bombs. And now, God helping us, we face the deep need of reconversion to some Christian confidence in spiritual forces, in education and persuasion, in the efficacy of good will, in the power of Christian faith and life to transform men and nations. That reconversion is going to be a job!

Long ago, outside Jerusalem, a man hung on a cross, so far as outward eye could see a pitiable failure if ever there was one, with nothing to count on except the appeal of his life and character, his divine love and sacrifice. Nothing to count on but that! Yet there on Calvary the supreme miracle of history took place. I have thought about it for a lifetime, and I cannot yet see how what happened there could happen. For that so fragile appeal of the spirit to the spirit has turned out to be tremendous, incredibly transforming, obdurate as granite in its endurance and, in its conquest of mankind's noblest souls, powerful beyond belief. Since then many an empire has tumbled down, but the influence of that life and character and sacrifice goes on. Believe it or not, there in the realm of spirit we find what lasts and triumphs in the end. The victories of physical force, however noisy and ostentatious, and however necessary we may think them, are temporary; only the spirit's victories that inwardly persuade and transform men, last. And we Christians are supposed to believe in this power of the spiritual forces, as Paul said, "divinely strong to demolish fortresses."

To be sure, I know that in this regard the war is far from being over. Still the nations trust in armies, navies, airplanes, bombs and all the rest. War is like a surgical operation; if you once start it you've got to finish it, at least to the point of sewing the patient up; you cannot suddenly stop it in the middle just because you discover that the patient needed, not an operation, but medical treatment. Thus it is going to take a long time to achieve the ethical reconversion we Christians pray for, from trust in violence to a really peaceful world. But if some here are thinking that such reconversion in the long run is not necessary, consider another scene, very different from Calvary. It is the deck of the battleship *Missouri*, in Yokohama Bay; the pomp and panoply of military power are there; and representing one of the most colossal victories in history, General MacArthur is speaking as Japan surrenders. He is not speaking about war but about peace, and, naming the endeavors made to achieve peace that have failed, he says: "We have had our last chance. If we do not now devise some greater and more equitable system Armageddon will be at our door. The problem basically is theological and involves a spiritual recrudescence and improvement of human character . . . It must be of the spirit if we are to save the flesh."

That, I think, is the most remarkable thing ever said at a ceremony of surrender concluding a great war. If someone here will not listen to the message of Calvary, thinking it too idealistic and visionary, will he listen to that word from the deck of a victorious battleship? The time is up, my friends. If we are to save the flesh now, we must win a victory for the spirit.

The reconversion of mind and emotion involved in this victory includes the overcoming of discouraged moods. This post-war era is discouraging. After two world wars to see the nations muffing the peace again is depressing. Polycarp, the Christian martyr, who died for his faith in Smyrna in 156 A.D., used to say, "My God! In what a century have you caused me to live!" I should say so!

Nevertheless, taking our situation so, we ourselves contribute to the disaster that will follow. We humans are a strange lot! We can be magnificent in war, keeping our faith in victory though one defeat follows another, and hanging on like bulldogs through thick and thin. Remember Winston Churchill when Britain faced her most hopeless days? "Let us . . . so bear ourselves that if the British Commonwealth and Empire lasts for a thousand years, men will still say, 'This was their finest hour.'" But when peace comes, and the first few months face us with discouragements, many are tempted to cave in and give up.

Consider the building of our own nation. The thirteen colonies were comparatively homogeneous, with the same language for the most part and, in general, the same heritage. Surely, their swift union might have been anticipated. Yet again and again in those early years a federal government seemed hopeless. Alexander Hamilton himself despaired of the Constitution and called it a "frail and worthless fabric." In 1829 John Randolph of Virginia said, "The country is ruined past redemption," and in 1832 Chancellor Kent of New York threw up the sponge, saying, "We are going to destruction." Had such disheartenment wrecked the Union, historians today would be saying, Union proved impossible, it could not be done. But it could be done—if—if enough people took, as they did take, thank God! the struggle for unity and peace as they had taken war, determined to win, cost what time, patience and sacrifice it might.

Such undiscouraged determination is indispensable now, and there is good ground for it. Between Russia and ourselves there is much to work on beside disagreement and distrust. No nation wants peace more than Russia does. With half her country to rebuild, says Major George Fielding Eliot, with forty thousand miles of railway to be laid, with twenty-five million people wanting roofs over their heads, with their whole industrial and social program to begin all over again where war interrupted it, Russia wants peace, and needs it as much as any nation on earth. We were not whipped at arms even when von Rommel hammered at the gates of Alexandria, and we are not whipped now in our fight for peace, though it will take long, long years of patient, undiscouraged continuance.

Moreover, reconversion to forward-looking spiritual militancy involves the overcoming of our reactionary attitudes. Let's get back, we are tempted to say; the old days were not perfect, but they were good old days compared with these. Not many Americans, to be sure, are arguing now for isolation in the old-fashioned sense; but who does not feel the rising emotional disgust with all this mess that international responsibility involves us in? If only we could get out from under it, let foreigners run their own unhappy affairs, while we make the most of our unravished land. So, whatever our heads may think about Wendell Willkie's *One World*, our emotions can become reactionary, disgusted with the cockpit of Europe and the insoluble problems of Asia, until we not only want our soldiers back from the ends of the earth, but wonder how much good our diplomats are doing there.

If we take our situation so, we are sunk, for we are in one of those places in history where there is no road back. We talk, for example, about not wanting to give up our national sovereignty, but so far as the great issues of war and peace are concerned, we have lost our national sovereignty already. It is no longer in our power, when a great war breaks, to decide whether we will go in or not. Again and again we have tried to stay out, and we can't. We are the most powerful industrial nation in the world, and the waging of war depends now upon industry. So, when Europe goes to war, the great question, and, as in this last war, the decisive question, looms—which side will get the product of American factories? One side will. Which? Thus from the very start, long before our armies march, we are in the war. We are up against it, we Americans. A little nation like Switzerland may still retain its sovereign right to remain neutral, but we never can. As we have proved so often that it is insane to doubt it, our power of choice has already gone, our sovereign right to go to war, or to stay out, has already vanished.

The only way, therefore, in which we can possibly retain any power to decide on war or no war, is to go forward into a world organization, in which we play the responsible part to which our strength entitles us.

This congregation is full of people, young people, old people, whose whole emotional and moral future depends on how they take these years of turmoil we are plunging into. The casualties of war, alas! do not stop when war does. A disastrous hurricane is always followed by tremendous seas and many a ship that survived the gale is swamped by the mountainous billows that come afterward. So many millions more will die of starvation that follows the war than died in war itself, and many too who stood up emotionally while the conflict was on, courageous and confident, will crack up in disillusionment or retreat into reactionary attitudes when they confront war's dismaying aftermath.

This is true of us civilians and it is true of you men and women of the fighting forces. So one naval officer wrote recently to an editor: "I lost my fear of death at Guadalcanal. I lost my best friend at Okinawa. I lost my leg at Iwo. And I lost my faith in American democracy after reading your article on displaced German persons. What *was* I fighting for?" That is a condensed history familiar in every war. Fighting men lose fear, lose their best friends, lose their own limbs and still are strong. But when the war is over and they see the consequence, they may lose faith.

Friends, the call now is for spiritual militancy, and the abiding facts are on our side. About a decade ago a German boy, under the influence of the youth movement, came home with expressions of contempt for Christianity and of admiration for the Nazis. His Christian parents were shocked, and protested as much as they dared, but the boy thought he saw the drift of the world's affairs. "Adolf Hitler," he said, "has become so big, and Jesus Christ has become so small." Well, sometimes it takes only a decade, sometimes it takes centuries; but the outcome is always the same. The Hitlers grow so big, and then they grow so small, and when the transient episode is over, Christ is still there, saying as of old: O Jerusalem, Jerusalem, hadst thou but known the things that belong unto thy peace!

[69]

Our Difficulty in Forgiving Our Enemies

THAT the forgiveness of enemies is basic in the teaching of Jesus is obvious, but many Christians are perplexed about its practice. Even when forgiveness is simply a personal affair it is often difficult, but in that case the arguments for it are clear and strong.

For one thing, the alternative to pardoning private wrong—bitterness, resentment, grudge bearing, vindictiveness—is one of the most self-destructive attitudes anyone can entertain. It may be true, as Sir Walter Scott said, that revenge is "the sweetest morsel to the mouth that ever was cooked in hell," but it almost always does more harm to the one who eats it than to anybody else, so that even on the ground of psychological good health one would plead with a wronged person, for his own sake, for a magnanimous, unresentful spirit. Moreover, we have learned to admire the forgiving spirit when we see it in others. A vindictive man no one really likes, whereas in such a man as Lincoln nothing more attracts us than his magnanimity.

With regard to private wrongs, therefore, we generally know that we ought to be forgiving, but now we face a public situation where our attitude toward our enemies, one of the world's major problems, is not so simple. Applied to the Nazis and the Japanese military party during the war Jesus' words seemed positively dangerous. Peter said to him, "Lord, how oft shall my brother sin against me, and I forgive him? until seven times? Jesus saith unto him, I say not unto thee, Until seven times; but, Until seventy times seven." How could that be applied to our public enemies?

Facing this problem, we Christians may well try to grasp afresh the real meaning of forgiveness. Oversimplification of words is a major peril in religion. A great soul uses a great word in a great sense, and then we lesser folk pick up the word, thin it out, water it down, sentimentalize it, until while we say verbally what the great soul said, we are not meaning what he meant. Nowhere is that process more evident than in our popular use of the word "forgiveness."

We commonly talk as though forgiveness were a one-way street on which a gracious spirit moves out, carrying pardon to all and sundry, no matter what they have done or what their attitude now is, whereas everywhere in the New Testament forgiveness is a two-way street on which penitence must move to meet the pardoning spirit before forgiveness can be consummated.

Say if we will that the father of the Prodigal was willing to forgive him. Indeed he was! He wanted nothing so much as to pardon that wayward son. But to say that he could forgive him, while that son, impenitent, reveled in the debauchery of the Far Country, is an inaccurate use of language. That father's heart, turbulent with desire to forgive, was blockaded, unable to pardon no matter how much he wanted to, until the conditions were fulfilled that alone make forgiveness possible. Then the time came when the younger son returned home, penitent. What an hour! The conditions of forgiveness were at last fulfilled; the dammed-up stream of a father's pardon released by the only thing that could release it—the penitence of the wrongdoer. Forgiveness is a much more serious process than our popular sentimentality makes it out to be.

It will not do, therefore, to pick out a few words of Jesus about forgiveness and leave the matter there. He did forgive, seventy times seven. He saw those first disciples meaning well, struggling toward the light, often blind to his truth, failing to catch his spirit, and seventy times seven he forgave them. But he met another kind of person too—hard as nails and cruel as hell, of whom he said that it were better that a great millstone should be hanged about his neck, and he be cast into the midst of the sea. "Whited sepulchres," he cried, of some men he saw, "which outwardly appear beautiful, but inwardly are full of dead men's bones, and of all uncleanness." If, then, someone says, Jesus contradicts himself, he is not forgiving, I answer, No, even when he was thus hottest in his invective he still was willing to forgive, and at the close of that most scathing philippic in ancient literature, Matthew's twenty-third chapter, where his condemnation is blistering, he cried, "O Jerusalem, Jerusalem, that killeth the prophets, and stoneth them that are sent unto her! how often would I have gathered thy children together, even as a hen gathereth her chickens under her wings, and ye would not!" Always willing to forgive he was, but even he could not forgive until the conditions were fulfilled—penitence, that alone brings to the pardoning spirit its release, and to forgiveness its consummation.

We commonly say that Jesus on the cross forgave his murderers, but that too is inaccurate. He did not forgive them; he prayed that God would: "Father, forgive them; for they know not what they do." That means, of course, that Jesus himself was willing to forgive, but even he could not escape the moral law, in accordance with which forgiveness is a game that two must play at, the one penitent, the other merciful. Well, Pilate and Caiaphas were not penitent, nor the gambling soldiers casting lots for Jesus' cloak at the foot of the cross. So our Lord prayed, as though to say, May they sometime be penitent, and then, Father, forgive them. Thus Luke reports a saying of Jesus: "If thy brother trespass against thee, rebuke him; and if he repent, forgive him." Apply that principle to our public situation now and no wonder we are perplexed. An appalling mass of impenitent brutality confronts us, by which the most ardent Christian desire to forgive is blocked.

The Christian who sees only one side of this matter may tell us that if our love were only deep and strong enough we could forgive everyone, but that attitude fails to take account of a puzzling paradox: namely, that Christian love itself often makes forgiveness most difficult. When a brute of a man mistreats a little child, suppose we love the child. That does not make it easy to forgive the brute; it makes it hard. To say that Jesus' love was so deep and strong that he found it easy to forgive everyone, misrepresents the facts. Jesus saw Dives cruelly mistreating Lazarus, and loving Lazarus he turned on Dives with terrific indignation. Today, thinking of the atrocities, the cold-blooded policies of torture and extermination, whose revelation has left us all stunned and horrified, suppose we love humanity, sensitively care for wronged and tormented men, women and children, the first effect of that is not to make forgiveness of the torturers easy, but to make it difficult. Not our hatred, but our love for the grossly wronged, demands that the wrongdoers be put out of business, justly punished, and the repetition of their cruelty made impossible. Take Jesus' life and teaching as a whole and that stern message, born not of vindictiveness at all, but of love for the oppressed and wronged, is there too.

Nevertheless, anyone can be resentful today, angrily calling for retribution. Surely there is something else, specifically Christian, that should characterize the disciples of Jesus. To this basic matter we now address ourselves. Of course there is a distinctively Christian attitude, and it roots back in what we have called the willingness to forgive. Always in Jesus, even on Calvary, was the desirous readiness to forgive, if only the door to it would open. What factors, we ask now, entered into that attitude, that made Christ, Christ, that produced the miracle of his redeeming saviorhood, and that we Christians deeply need to learn from him?

For one thing, to Jesus the ultimate, long-range objective was always, not the punishment of the evildoer, but his redemption. Jesus never doubted the necessity of punishment for men and nations and, child of the Hebrew prophets as he was, some of the most tremendous statements ever made about retribution came from his lips. But never did his thought stop there; always his long-range objective was the redemption of the sinner.

Zacchaeus had a bad record, and Jesus felt that. An extortioner, misusing the power of his position to fleece the poor, Zacchaeus violated everything Jesus stood for. The Master was not easy on him. Zacchaeus had to repent, make restitution, restore fourfold what he had stolen; but what made Christ's meeting with him distinctive was that beyond retribution Jesus' eyes were fixed on the ultimate objective—the redemption of Zacchaeus.

Can we Christians now supply this element in our present situation? The evil Germany has brought upon the world is appalling, and the necessity of stern dealing, just retribution, the prevention of such evil's repetition, is obvious. The trouble is that popular thinking commonly stops there. Put Christ into this picture, however, and you know what he would be thinking about: the ultimate saving of Germany. To call that unrealistic is nonsense; it is about the most realistic thing we can be undertaking, now that Germany is conquered. It will never be well with Europe and the world until Germany is redeemed to a constructive role among the nations. Difficult? I should say so! But nothing will be well until it is achieved. Sixty to eighty million Germans in the center of Europe were a problem before our military victory, and they are still a problem, whose final, conclusive solution lies not in their punishment alone, inevitable as it is, but in their re-education, their redemption, their return to the family of nations. If Christ were here, that long-range, ultimate objective would be at the very center of his thought and purpose.

In achieving that, the nation as such can go about so far, but to the Christian Church it presents a supreme challenge. Already the World Council of Churches is at work upon it. We Christians must re-establish fraternal relationships with our German brethren. We too commonly forget that it was German Christians who fought Hitler first—thousands of Protestant pastors there going to his concentration camps because they would not crook the knee. To team up with all the saving elements in Germany and work for her redemption is at once our duty and our privilege, with momentous consequence dependent on our success in doing it.

We older folk remember the Boxer Rebellion and the atrocities practiced by the Boxers then. Our anger was hot, our call for retribution stern. Well, when the Boxers were liquidated, this nation did something distinctively Christian, returning the Boxer indemnity to provide scholarships for Chinese students in this country; but the Christian churches went deeper yet. A missionary was brutally slain by the Boxers. His son went back to China as a missionary to serve in the same village where his father had been murdered. Believe me, that did something that no other power on earth can ever do! Such is the redemptive business of the Christian churches, and they must be about it now.

Listen to these words—I can hardly credit them—"There must be no bitterness in the reconstructed world. No matter what we have undergone and suffered, we must try to forgive those who injured us." Mme. Chiang Kai-shek said that. How could she say it? Yet that is Christianity, not soft, not sentimental, but hardheadedly keeping in the center of attention the long-range ultimate objective, without the achievement of which all victories and all punishments are vain—the re-education and redemption of our foes, in the end, as Lincoln said, destroying our enemies by making them our friends.

This leads us to a further truth we need to learn from Jesus. This willingness to forgive, even before forgiveness itself is possible, springs from a deep conviction that if we are to be forgiven ourselves we must be ready to forgive others. Throughout Jesus' teaching runs this emphasis on the law of reciprocity: "Forgive us our trespasses, As we forgive those who trespass against us." "When ye stand praying, forgive, if ye have ought against any: that your Father also which is in heaven may forgive you your trespasses." That law of reciprocity in forgiveness is a searching matter to face now.

From the Master's point of view we are all involved in guilt. No easy matter that for us, the victorious nations, now to confront, but it is true, and to see its truth one need not minimize the Nazi crimes at all. They were atrocious. Our racial prejudice in the United States is vile, but we have never made it a governmental policy, backing up a monstrous program of cold-blooded torture and extermination; and such calculated barbarity as the Nazis deliberately perpetrated on millions of hapless, tormented victims, I agree could not have happened here. Nevertheless, let us face the fact that this atrocious cruelty is the fruit of war, that it is war which releases it and makes its worst expressions possible, and that all the nations by what we have done and left undone share a common responsibility for war's continuance in our international life! We cannot honestly escape the inclusive sense of guilt. "All we like sheep have gone astray."

One major effect of these last few years on some of us has been to make us take sin more seriously than we ever took it before. From all that cheap teaching about the mere relativity of right and wrong that prevailed a few years ago, we have revolted in disgust. Some things are everlastingly right and some things everlastingly wrong, and sin can be, and visibly is, hellish—that should be obvious now. When one, however, thus takes sin seriously, one cannot push it all off on our enemies; especially in the perpetuation of war, we all have sinned, and need to be forgiven.

See what we ourselves have come to in the prosecution of war! We have justified the use of atomic bombs on Hiroshima and Nagasaki, but the ethical implication of that justification we commonly have refused to face. It means that we accept as the sole criterion of conduct in war the efficiency of any destructive weapon to win victory. All other standards of right and wrong are pushed aside. Anything is right that wins military victory. Mass murder of whole metropolitan populations is right if it is effective—such is the meaning of our justification of atomic warfare. That involves the scrapping of mankind's ethical gains for untold generations, the abolishment of every moral standard the best conscience of the race ever has set up; it means that nothing is wrong that destroys an enemy, that anything is right that wins a war. We who have come to that deplorable condition of thought and practice are in no position to wash our hands in innocency and call others guilty.

Far from being sentimental, this is stark, unpleasant realism, and we had better face it. Whatever constructive and saving results come from the United Nations will be born of this penitent mood and temper, all the nations needing to repent together, amend their ways, and turn their faces in unison toward a new kind of world. And whatever results from the United Nations are least constructive and most full of peril for mankind's future, will spring from the lack of that mood and temper, as though we did not need to repent and be forgiven. "Forgive us our trespasses, As we forgive those who trespass against us," is a searching prayer today!

This attitude we have been pleading for, this Christian willingness to forgive, has been about the most spiritually redeeming factor in mankind's history. Our personal experience of it began with our mothers. Often they could not fully bestow forgiveness on us in our impenitence, but always behind our unrepentant stubbornness we knew that our mothers' desirous, outgoing willingness to forgive was there, if only we would open the door to it, and that was one of the most powerful, saving influences that played upon our youth.

What salvation is there for the world without it? Lacking it, see what history is reduced to! One nation hates another, and the other hates back, and that hate is answered by hate again and that hatred by hatred in return, and so the endless cycle goes on—resentment met only by resentment, wrongdoing by wrongdoing. They bomb our cities, murder our children, destroy our hospitals, churches, schools, libraries and homes, and we do the same to them. Then, angry, they plan revenge, and we in turn make ready to fight back; and so on and on forever. Something transcending hatred, surpassing revenge or even just punishment, must enter in if we are to be saved; and the essence of Christ's saviorhood was this miraculous extra—love even toward enemies, constructive, intelligent good will, determined to break the awful sequence of hatred answered by hatred, and so to save the world.

I am not saying that this is easy, either to believe in or to practice. Do not suppose that I find it easy! But without it there is no hope for the world, and it works—sometimes at least it works. There is a legend of the early church, so ancient that there may be truth in it, that the centurion who presided at our Lord's crucifixion was named Longinus, the man who seeing in what spirit Christ died, cried, "Truly this was the Son of God," and, so the legend runs, that centurion himself was so deeply moved by what he saw at Calvary that he became a Christian and was at last a martyr for the Christian cause. That kind of conquest is the only ultimate victory, and nothing but Christ's kind of love can win it. Some people think that the hymn, *The Son of God Goes Forth to War*, is militant, and so it is, but listen to it:

> "Like him, with pardon on his tongue,
> In midst of mortal pain,
> He prayed for them that did the wrong:
> Who follows in his train?"

The Impossibility of Being Irreligious

WHEN Paul preached on Mars Hill in Athens he opened his address by saying: "Men of Athens, I observe at every turn that you are a most religious people." That is Dr. Moffatt's translation and it represents, I think, what Paul really meant. Our more familiar versions use the word "superstitious," but Paul in Athens was dealing with a deeper matter than that word stands for. The Greeks were "a most religious people."

Paul was facing there an obvious fact in the ancient world —the universality of religion. What he said in Athens could have been said anywhere, from Egypt with its stately temples, to Britain with its druid shrines. Nowhere would he have found irreligion.

In our modern world many suppose that situation to be outgrown. We deal, so we think, with downright irreligion, materialism, atheism, denying all gods whatsoever. Today, however, I share with you the conviction that far from our escaping the situation Paul confronted on Mars Hill, only its form has changed, and that whether we like it or not, we are all most religious people. Paul was not complimenting the Athenians when he called them that. He was confronting them with an austere fact: religion inescapable; religion immensely powerful; religion, the thing men do practically believe in and give themselves to, inevitable; and therefore all men faced with this unavoidable choice—what kind of religion will you have?

The idea that a man can be irreligious is so commonly taken for granted that it may require patient thought to adjust ourselves to the idea that he can never be. Yet look at our world today! Were the Nazis irreligious? Upon the contrary, they saw that they could never do what they were determined to do on the basis of the Jewish-Christian faith, and so they set themselves to find a substitute religion. They found it. Alfred Rosenberg was its prophet. They restored, in effect, the Nordic tribal deities; they said they wanted "no God but Germany"; they put the Fuehrer in the place of Christ; they glorified this religion in impressive ritual, confirmed it in a fanatical fellowship, and gave it a devotion that makes us Christians wish we could match it in our loyalty to him whom we call Lord. Hitler could never have done what he did had he not made of his cause a religion. As Konrad Heiden in his study of the Fuehrer's rise to power puts it: "Hitler was able to enslave his own people because he seemed to give them something that even the traditional religions could no longer provide; the belief in a meaning to existence beyond the narrowest self-interest."

As we try to understand the importance of this truth, that in ways good, bad or indifferent, man is inescapably religious, consider first that it is rooted in man's psychological make-up. We commonly use the word "faith," as a synonym for "religion," employing the two words interchangeably, and we are right. A man's real religion is what he does verily put his faith in and give his devotion to.

The consequence of that, however, at once confronts us. Faith is a capacity in human nature that we cannot get rid of; we exercise it all the time on something or other. One man in our New York community we would naturally call irreligious. He certainly does not believe in God. "I am," he writes contemptuously, "for all religions equally, as all impress me as being equally hollow." But just at the point where we begin to think, Here is really an irreligious man, he says this: "To me, pleasure and my own personal happiness . . . are all I deem worth a hoot." So that is what he has faith in! He does have an inner shrine where he worships—himself. He does have an altar—not to an unknown god but to his own ego, put first in this whole universe as all he deems worth a hoot. That is his religion.

All through this congregation are folk, I suspect, who habitually think of religion as a matter of their free election; they can be religious or not, as they choose. But that is a delusion. Every last man and woman of us puts faith in something, gives devotion to something, is coerced by a psychological necessity to make a religion of something. Is not the conclusion urgent? Thus compelled to be religious—with momentous consequence to ourselves and to our influence in the world, let us get the best religion we can find, the very best!

No one, I trust, will be confused by our use of one word about so many different things—not Buddhism, Mohammedanism and Christianity alone, but Nazism, and egocentricity—just as Paul used it about an idolatrous altar in Athens. Science, so it has been said, is the art of giving the same name to different things; that is to say, considering black coal, white paper, red apples, green leaves, and colorless gasoline, it takes science to reveal that they all alike are chiefly carbon. This morning let us exercise that same kind of insight about religion! The mightiest forces in human life—faith in Christ, faith in the Fuehrer, the self-committal that makes Luther say, "Here stand I, I cannot otherwise," and the self-committal that makes an egocentric adore himself, the worship that prays to the Father who seeth in secret, and the worship that builds an altar to an unknown God—all alike spring from a profound, ineradicable religious necessity in man to believe in something, give himself to something, belong to something.

Even before we go further with this matter does it not come home to some of us here? You are religious, it says; you can never be irreligious; for your own soul's sake and for the world's sake, face the question—what kind of religion have you got?

Consider now that this truth is not only rooted in our psychological constitution but is amply illustrated in history. Some things, so history reveals, can be outgrown, but others are elemental, ineradicable—like agriculture. Men may pursue agriculture in primitive fashion, scratching the ground with sharp sticks, and eking out a pitiful subsistence, or they may discover the chemistry of soil and bring to their farming all the aids and implements that science knows; but still, of necessity, they go on with agriculture, and the only cure for bad agriculture is good agriculture—never giving agriculture up.

So is it with religion as history records the story. We contrast the might of the Roman Empire with the seeming feebleness of Jesus' cause that day they crucified him on Calvary, and we marvel at the miracle that while Rome fell, the man of Nazareth has gone on, the most influential force in the spiritual history of man. That is a miracle, incredible to contemporaries, but not so strange as this other one. When Jesus was crucified there was at Delphi in Greece a shrine to which seekers had come for ages, to get the oracles of the gods. Older than the Roman Empire, it appeared likely to outlast the Empire—a religion so seemingly permanent that when it began to dwindle men could not believe their eyes. Two generations after Christ Plutarch wrote that men had been "in anguish and fear lest Delphi should lose its glory of three thousand years." Well, Delphi did peter out, but it was not irreligion that ended it; another religion ended it, although to pit the Christ on Calvary against the authority and splendor of Delphi would at first have seemed insane.

There we face a universal truth of history: the only cure for religion is religion—never irreligion.

Has someone here this morning been off religion? For one reason or another, you are off religion. Friend, you are right about one thing: there is a lot of dangerous, superstitious, morally harmful religion, but the cure is not where you are headed. The only remedy for sick religion is healthy religion—never irreligion. You had better come over and help us. The issue is critical today. As a friend of mine put it: "When times are at their worst, we need religion at its best." How crucially we need it now—great religion, intelligent, ethical, unifying, building foundations under our democratic faith in the worth of personality, in the essential equality of all souls before God, in the right of persons as God's children to liberty, and in the eternal purpose, as this world is now one neighborhood, to make it as well one brotherhood. You had better come over and help us. The only cure for bad religion is great religion—never irreligion.

Dr. Shotwell, Professor of History at Columbia writes: "Religion moves, vast and potent, in the world today. One must be blind, indeed, not to see the evidences of its power in both the structure and the movement of our modern world." Granted, much of this vast and potent religion is evil in its consequence. Once more, as in Athens, Paul would look at it with a sad heart, but he would know still that the cure is not negative, but positive. "What therefore ye worship in ignorance," he said, "this I set forth unto you."

Consider now that this truth, rooted in our very nature and illustrated in our race's history, confronts us in our churches. It is easy enough to understand why a man gives up the church. Quite apart from the antiquated nonsense sometimes talked in churches, the trivial, negative moralisms that sometimes flourish there, the conventionality that makes their observances futile, and the hollow monotony of some churches that talk about religion once a week but do nothing about it the rest of the time, is the accusation that none of us can dodge: the appalling sectarianism of our churches, making of religion, that ought to be mankind's most unifying influence, one of the world's most divisive forces instead.

Sometimes a preacher, pleading that statesmen must build an international order that will bring peace, wonders why somebody does not shout Hypocrite! at him, saying, You demand that statesmen create unity among these warring nations, but you have never been able to do that even in your churches that preach one God and all men brethren. I can think up an answer—of a sort. Look at our divorce rate—we have not learned how to keep peace in our own families. Look at our churches— we have not learned how to get together around the altar of our one God. Nevertheless, unable satisfactorily to create peace even in these smaller groups, we still do face the necessity of creating peace in the world at large. This is the irony of our problem, and it cannot be dodged because it is difficult. No such answer, however, that anyone can think up, obscures the fact that over much of our organized religion Paul would shake a sad head as he did at Athens.

At that point, however, I remember someone most of all worth remembering. What Jesus said about the churches of his day was blistering. If I should tear loose this morning and use all the language I have sometimes thought of in disgust with the faults of the churches, I would not approach the awful language he used about the organized religion of his day: hypocrites, whited sepulchres, blind guides, serpents, generation of vipers. The mild and gentle Christ was talking there about the church of his day, but note this, he was attacking the evils of the church, not in the name of irreligion but in the name of great religion.

A momentous difference distinguishes those two attitudes. Never mix them up! I put it to you—someone here in rebellion against the church. We are not now denying a single thing you say about the church. Jesus himself said worse. But face frankly what the meaning of your rebellion is. Does it mean: Out of the church toward irreligion? That will not get you or anyone else anywhere. If men and women who, like you, feel deeply the church's failures, leave the church, that will mean, not that there will be no churches, but only that there will be worse and worse churches. Another attitude, however, has produced the best in the church's history, from the Master himself, to Luther and Wesley, and all their kin. They too, attacked the failures of the church, but not in the name of irreligion; they spoke in the name of great religion.

You had better come over and help us. The question in America is not whether we shall have churches or not, but only what kind of churches we shall have. And we cannot stand having bad churches, any more than we can stand having bad homes and schools. Homes, schools, churches—these are the central builders of the nation's character, and when times are at their worst, we need them at their best. In that sense, too, we are "a most religious people."

Rooted in our very nature, exemplified in our race's history, confronting us in our churches, this truth we are dealing with finds its most telling illustration in our own personal experience. Whoever we are, whatever our background or belief, we have never succeeded very well in being irreligious. Something from the deeps of life is forever breaking through to disturb the ir-religion we try to settle down in.

Even in ordinary times this is true. As Browning said, picturing a man trying to be contentedly irreligious,

> "Just when we are safest, there's a sunset-touch,
> A fancy from a flower-bell, some one's death,
> A chorus-ending from Euripides."

So, even in peaceful eras our so-called irreligion is constantly disturbed by intimations of a spiritual world that materialism never can explain. Now, however, the world is facing paganism, triumphant and frightening. Many who a few years ago were in revolt against religion find themselves, for a new and cogent reason, instinctively rebelling against irreligion.

Rebellion against anything is interesting and exciting; professors of irreligion have long enjoyed it with zest and gusto; so long as religion was here to rebel against, it was fun to attack it. But then, atheistic communism rose. Then Hitler came, and nazism made its announcement: "The Sermon on the Mount is, according to Nordic sentiment, an ethic for cowards and idiots." Then total war broke, and the world saw what thoroughgoing paganism means when it gets going. Am I wrong in thinking that the deep instinct of revolt in mankind against intolerable things is now changing its direction? Granted, the mistakes of religion! It is not against that, at its best and in its deepest meanings, we now rebel, but against this intolerable heathenism that denies God and everything that he and his Christ ever stood for.

The story runs that before the war a Frenchman in Paris harbored strong anti-Semitic prejudices. Then the Nazis came and took over Paris and that Frenchman saw the ghastly things that anti-Semitism really means. The other day, we read, on a street in Paris that a Frenchman, meeting a Jew whom he knew, greeted him cordially. "Friend," he said, "these Nazis have taken everything away from me, even my anti-Semitism." I should say so! Fools that we are, we often have to see what we stand for carried to its logical, intolerable conclusion before we recognize what it really means. I am hoping that before we are through today some here may be saying, This prevalent paganism has taken away from me, not only my anti-Semitism but my complacence about those who make a religion of the worst, my easygoing idea that we can displace God with something less than God, and get away with it, my mild admiration for Christ as though he were only a lovely ideal for those who like him. Anyone, I should suppose, with his eyes open, must be in revolt now, not against Christianity—not Christianity at its best—but against paganism.

In wide areas of our personal and social life in this country and in mankind's life as a whole, the revolt against religion has succeeded, the Christian God has been banished, and Christian principles of life have been thrown out. But look who's here, to take their place! Venus, and Bacchus, and mendacious Mercury, and Mars! We of this generation are back where the New Testament stood, facing prevalent paganism, with an urgency in the Christian gospel that many of us never felt before.

This situation commonly confronts us most poignantly in our homes. Some parents are queer folk, off religion for years, seemingly well content, and then the children come and what they thought they did not need themselves they begin to wish the children had—a share in the great spiritual faith and tradition of the race. One father was like that; his son went off to school, to Phillips Andover, and the father went with him on the first trip and attended chapel service at the opening session. When the service was over he came down the aisle, the evidence of tears too obvious to be hidden, and said to the principal, "Mr. Stearns, as you can see I have been making something of a fool of myself this morning, but I am not sorry. I am not much on this church business. In fact, I don't think I have been inside a church for years although I was brought up in an old-fashioned Christian New England home and know better. But this morning when I saw those five hundred heads bowed like one man at the beginning of your prayer something gripped me inside and I cried like a baby and I am not ashamed. So long as my boy is in your school I am going to be present at every chapel service I can possibly attend." So, like all mankind, we moderns are not a great success at being irreligious.

If thus by our deepest nature we are made for religion, let us get it at its best! We face a world where many are making a religion of the worst. Unless enough of us make a religion of the best, we are sunk. I present Christ to you. I am not thinking now of complicated theologies about him, but of Christ himself, the revelation of the Divine, and the savior of the human. He is the best we know. He is great religion. In our deepest hours we know that were the world really to accept him, be devotedly loyal to him, then the world would be saved.

Some personal consequences ought to come from this service. I want something to happen here—people, namely, who for their own sakes, for the sake of those they love, for the world's sake, will make a real religion of the Christ.

Why We Believe in God

ONE of the astounding facts about Christ's crucifixion is that it has been for Christians the supreme revelation of God's love—"God commendeth his own love toward us, in that, while we were yet sinners, Christ died for us"—and yet concentrated in that crucifixion are all the factors that make it most difficult to believe in God at all, to say nothing of his love. What makes faith in God difficult is life's injustice, its cruelty, what Keats called "the giant agony of the world," and there on Calvary you have all that. They flogged Christ, pressed thorns into his brow, spat on him, crucified him—*crudelissimum deterrimumque supplicium,* Cicero called crucifixion, the most cruel and terrific punishment—and there, having nailed him to the cross, they watched him die in agony. The horror of the Nazi prison camps has seemed to us intolerable even to imagine, but here it is on Calvary—barbaric torture of history's noblest personality. Yet Christian faith has seen in that crucifixion the supreme revelation of God's love. How can that be?

For many in these days it is not easy to believe in God. Go through this congregation, saying its prayers, singing its hymns, looking so religious and worshipful, but what secret doubts lurk, what questions rise, what agnosticism confronts us deep within when we try to imagine a good God in such a world! It is not some new theoretical arguments that have disturbed our faith; the brutality and horror of the world's evil and the agony of the peoples have crashed through all the comfortable safeguards we ordinarily erect against their impact, and the cry is wrung from us, How can there be a God, much less a good God, in such a world?

Indeed, some here may have gone far beyond doubt into thoroughgoing disbelief. God, they say, is a kind of Santa Claus

[88]

we humans in our need of comfort have sentimentally invented, to think about and pray to and hope for blessings from; and looking at us Christians they feel like saying: Children, there is no Santa Claus at all! Look at the world and see!

Some ideas of God do lay themselves open to such disbelief. God certainly is no Santa Claus. The cross, however, where Christian faith starts, does not in the least suggest Santa Claus —nothing more damnable than that ever done on earth! "A terrible thing is life," said Socrates. Indeed it is, and never more so than on Calvary. Yet there Christian faith has seen God commending his love toward us. What can one make of that paradox?

The cross is thus the epitome of our deepest problem. There you have the very worst and the very best—both there—with the question rising, which are we going to put our faith in? Which goes deeper and reveals the more truly the ultimate nature of things? Let us face that issue! You who want to cry that this world is dreadful, do not pull your punches about that! It is dreadful; and there on Calvary is the essence of its dreadfulness: cruel torture, the innocent in agony, evil triumphant, and the whole affair, to outward seeming, a senseless horror. Say the worst you feel about life, call this earth, as John Stuart Mill did, an "odious scene of violence and tyranny," and you are still far within the compass of the historic Christian faith. That faith has always started with Calvary, where life was at its dreadfulest and worst, but there, where man's evil was at its worst, Christian faith has seen the good God supremely revealing himself. Facing the worst and the best at Calvary, man's sin and Christ's saviorhood, the Christian faith says, Which will you put your faith in as revealing the Eternal? You must choose.

Consider, in the first place, that we indeed must choose. I know all about agnosticism, and to how many it seems a place of neutral retreat. We neither believe in God, nor disbelieve, men say; we do not know. But that is a deceptive neutrality. Real faith in God is a positive matter—you either have it or you don't. To believe in a good God, in a divine origin for life, purpose in it, destiny ahead of it, to hear the stars

> "For ever singing as they shine,
> 'The Hand that made us is divine,'"

and deep within ourselves to feel the companionship of the Eternal Spirit, the Unseen Friend, such faith is a positive matter. You either have it or you miss it. If a man is an atheist, he hasn't got it, but if a man is an agnostic he hasn't got it either. Positive faith in God is something we either have, or haven't.

Surely a man can segregate what he calls his mind from the rest of himself, and, in his mind alone, can decline to say either yes or no to God. He can hold his judgment in suspense. But he cannot hold his life in suspense; that gets made up one way or the other; he either lives with a positive, sustaining, triumphant faith in God or he does not, and the agnostic misses that just as much as the atheist.

Like it or not, life is full of such forced decisions. A man can love and trust his wife, and deepening with the years such love and trust can be a glorious experience. A man either has that experience or he has not. If, as the alternative, he distrusts his wife he has missed it. Yes, and if he tries to be agnostic about his wife, saying, I neither trust nor distrust her, I suspend judgment as to whether she is trustworthy or not, he has missed it too. In all such vital matters there is no escape into neutrality. Life presents us with forced decisions.

At Calvary one confronts this forced issue about God. Everything that most makes men disbelieve in God is there; everything that most makes men believe in God is there. I can stand before Calvary and, looking at one aspect of it, cry, How can there be a good God? And I can stand before Calvary and, looking at the other aspect of it, cry, Such character, such sacrificial love can be no accidental outcome of ruthless matter; behind such goodness is an eternal source, as surely as behind the sunshine is the sun. But what I cannot do at Calvary is find any neutrality to which I can retreat. Life gets made up one way or the other. Still the classic words of Pascal are true: "This however is certain, either that God is, or that he is not; there is no medium point . . . You must wager; this is not a matter of choice; you are committed, and not to wager that God is, is to wager that he is not. Which side then do you take?"

Some of us have made our choice and do believe in God, in part because that character upon the cross and his sacrifice have done things to us and to the world that we are sure cannot be explained merely by protons and electrons going it blind.

Indeed, many things in this universe seem downright inexplicable by any such atheistic formula. A visitor, coming out of the Planetarium in this city, said to a friend, "Man, there is more than chance behind all that; there is mind in that." It certainly seems so. As a very young boy I used to think that the waving of the branches caused the wind. Why not? Whenever the branches wave the wind blows; the wind never does blow except when the branches wave. Is not that the simplest explanation—to account for the invisible by the movements of the visible? But believe it or not, the invisible wind comes first; even in the physical world the great causations come from the unseen.

Carry that analogy deeper. The New Testament is utterly inexplicable without its physical factors—the paper it is printed on, the type it is set in, the presses that print it. The physical is indispensable to the New Testament, but the creative cause of the New Testament, its ultimate fount and origin, go far back behind the physical into the invisible realm of mind and spirit. The more one knows about this universe the more that analogy holds. When a materialist says, as one did say, "All events are due to the interaction of matter and motion acting by blind necessity," my mind cries, That is childish! That is believing in magic! To explain Christ and all that Christ stands for by matter and motion acting by blind necessity is like thinking that the waving branches cause the wind, or explaining John's Gospel by the type it is set with, or saying that Einstein's intellect is caused by blind atoms following paths of least resistance in his brain. No! You cannot get that kind of rabbit out of any such hat!

What troubles most of us, however, is not so much the arguments of skeptical philosophy, as the awful facts, shown up in a scene like Calvary—life's cruelty, its brutal torture of the innocent, its senseless, wicked agony such as our eyes look upon today. Well, let's face it! If we start by believing in the best at Calvary, in Christ and his love as the revelation of the Eternal, if we say God is like that, we do face a mystery—the mystery of evil. How explain that? Why does God allow that? But suppose we reverse the process. Suppose we start with the worst at Calvary, the ruthless brutality there, and believe in that as the revelation of the ultimate truth of things—have we escaped mystery? My soul! We have run headlong into it, the most inexplicable of all mysteries: how, in a world with nothing but ruthless physical power at the heart of things, can one explain Christ and all that is Christlike in the world—friendship and beauty and creative intelligence and sacrificial love? There is a mystery—to get such things out of ruthless matter going it blind! Let us stop thinking that if we deny God we escape mystery; we run headlong into it in its most insoluble form.

One of Doolittle's flyers spent years in a Japanese prison camp, where he was flogged and starved. Yet listen to him, an American sergeant, Jacob DeShazer: "They were ignorant and mean," he says about his Japanese captors, "but, we thought, there was some good in them. The only way to develop that goodness would be by understanding and education—not by brutally mistreating them as they were doing to us. You can smile if you want to, but it made sense to me in that prison camp, and it still does. So I'm going to a missionary school for training and then I'm going to return to Japan and spend the rest

of my life there, teaching the importance of love among men."
That spirit too is in the world. Only a little of it, I know, but
still, it took only one footprint on Robinson Crusoe's island to
show that someone had been there. You could not explain that
footprint as the accidental impact of the waves upon the sand.
Someone had been there. And we cannot explain that kind of
spirit as the chance result of atoms going it blind—not by a long
sea mile, we can't! I for one choose not the ruthlessness at
Calvary, but the man on the cross there as the revelation of
the Eternal.

Another factor in the crucifixion constrains us to believe in
God, namely, the astonishing way that scene on Calvary came
out. It was appalling then; but now,

> "In the cross of Christ I glory,
>   Towering o'er the wrecks of time"—

millions sing that!

Here is a mystery requiring more than a materialistic philosophy to explain: the fact, namely, that so often the worst
turns the best in the end, a power and providence appear in life,
as though God indeed made even the wrath of men to serve
him. I am not pleading for sentimental optimism, as though to
say that everything always comes out all right—one cannot get
easygoing optimism out of Calvary. But I am remembering how
Pilate and Caiaphas went home that night, their vile work done,
that troublesome carpenter from Nazareth all finished, slain as
a felon, with the imprint of imperial Rome's condemnation on
him; and I am facing the fact that long since Rome has fallen
and Caesar gone, that Pilate and Caiaphas are the accursed now,
that Christ's life divine with its unearthly glory still is here,
the most haunting, fascinating figure in man's history, and that
cross of shame the symbol of salvation. That kind of thing just
cannot happen in a world where nothing is creative except blind

matter. That advertises a living providence, a guiding mind, a power beyond the power even of man's evil.

History's great agonies that made men deny God have often produced results that made men glorify God. Commonly in retrospect the world's troublous eras look far different from the way they looked when men were in the midst of them. "No chastening," says the New Testament, "for the present seemeth to be joyous, but grievous: nevertheless afterward it yieldeth the peaceable fruit of righteousness." I have read that verse hundreds of times but only the other day did the momentous meaning of those two words strike home: *"nevertheless afterward."* What a difference retrospect makes! Pharaoh towers over Moses until the disparity between them is ridiculous—nevertheless afterward! Babylon crushes Judea until the catastrophe is complete and terrible—nevertheless afterward! Where is Babylon? Where has not the influence of the great Isaiah gone? Pilate crucifies Christ, and evil hideously triumphs over righteousness—nevertheless afterward!

There is something in this universe besides matter and motion. There is something here that justifies Carlyle in saying, "No Lie can live for ever"; and Shakespeare in saying,

> "There's a divinity that shapes our ends,
> Rough-hew them how we will";

and Lowell in saying,

> "Truth forever on the scaffold, Wrong
> forever on the throne,—
> Yet that scaffold sways the future."

At our deepest, we believe that. As one of our fighting men back from the war said, "I do not believe I could have gone on but for my conviction that honor and decency belong on top in life." So! But that is no description of a godless world; only in a world with moral meaning at the center do honor and decency essentially belong on top. Such faith in God we need today—no soft bed to lie on, but an Eternal Purpose to co-operate with and be backed up by—and in these dismaying times I, for one, thank God that this strong faith is mine, to live and die with. The world is discouraging, but by God's grace some day, about our crisis now, like a great bell tolling those two words will again be heard —nevertheless afterward!

This, then, is the issue of the matter: on Calvary we come face to face, not so much with an argument as with a fact, a personality, a character, and as Dean Inge put it, "A character cannot be confuted." Arguments we can confute. Argument for argument we can debate it out, but when we are all done arguing, a great character is still there, not to be confuted or denied. So Christ confronts us. He is either an accident or a revelation, one or the other. An accident of purposeless matter going it blind— you may call him that if you can believe anything so utterly incredible; or else he is the revelation of something everlastingly so at the heart of things.

Some of us have had experiences with him deep within ourselves and in the lives of our friends, not to be confuted or denied. When King Arthur came to the Round Table where his knights were seated, Tennyson says,

"I beheld
From eye to eye thro' all their Order flash
A momentary likeness of the King."

That we too have seen in the spirits of men where Christ has come, a momentary likeness of the king—temptations conquered, evil habits overthrown, trouble surmounted, character transformed, social progress achieved, saviorhood not to be confuted or denied.

Such salvation we and the world we live in critically need today. It is a humbling experience for men and nations to acknowledge the need of being saved, but we surely face it. Military victory notoriously begets pride. After every victory it is the defeated who are restless, dissatisfied, rebellious, demanding change, while the conquerors are tempted to settle back, proud, self-satisfied, reactionary. America, never noted for its humility, is thus tempted now. Long ago Ralph Waldo Emerson said: "Your American eagle is very well. Protect it here and abroad. But beware of the American peacock." Surely the American peacock had better do no strutting now! We are in the same case with our allies—yes, and our enemies—one world, desperately needing to be saved.

Some nontheistic Humanist may say, What has God to do with this? Let us put our intelligence to work and save ourselves; faith in God is an opiate; it lulls men to sleep; believers put the responsibility off on God, when only we can save ourselves. To which I answer, What do you mean, faith in God an opiate? Faith in a God of righteousness, and of forward-moving purpose, in alliance with whose will we can work out our salvation, is no opiate, but the most challenging, stimulating, sustaining faith that mankind knows. The opiate that kills the hopes and drains the energies of men is cynicism. To feel that life has no divine origin, no divine meaning, no divine destiny—that is the opiate. What is the use, men say, nothing matters; we are the transient accidents of protons and electrons going it blind; there is no ultimate meaning in life. That view of life lets a man off from all serious responsibility. What can he do? If nothing matters, he does not matter. The honest-to-goodness fact is that in the actual experience of men cynicism, skepticism, disillusionment, are the opiates that deaden hope, drain courage, and exhaust the energies of men.

With faith in God, however, one's whole view of life is altered. Fellow-workers with the Eternal Purpose, we can draw on eternal resources. One by one, our inward lives can be re-enforced, and when in public affairs all goes wrong still,

> "Though this world, with devils filled,
> Should threaten to undo us
> We will not fear, for God hath willed
> His truth to triumph through us."

That is no opiate, but hope, and power, and stimulus and courage!

Some years ago a little church on the coast of England was ruined in a hurricane. The congregation thought themselves unable to rebuild. Then one day a representative of the British Admiralty came to the clergyman to ask if they intended to reconstruct the church. The clergyman explained why they could not do it. "Well," said the representative of the British Navy, "if you do not rebuild the church, we will. That spire is on all our charts and maps. It is the landmark by which the ships of the seven seas steer their course." A true parable, that! Never more than now, when the souls of men need divine help, stable and secure, strong, sustaining and empowering, was the church's message needed.

Take your choice! You can never make a more momentous decision. I believe in the ruthless Pilate and the treacherous Judas as the revelation of the Eternal—no! you do not really believe that. God was in Christ rather, in Christ there on Calvary, reconciling the world unto himself.

Finding Unfailing Resources

THESE days we are living through make a heavy demand on our strength. Action, output, work—to this energetic side of our lives, our time appeals. And because the church must and should feel the generation's characteristic needs, it is Christianity's active aspects that Sunday after Sunday we naturally think about. Our Christian responsibilities and obligations, what we should do and stand for and sacrificially bring to pass—this is the staple of our preaching. Yes, but a tree must have roots if it is to have branches. The Hudson River cannot bear the nation's commerce and its Navy unless it has unfailing sources. Even an airplane, mechanical though it is, with all its powers of flight and speed, is useless without ground service. The more the output, the greater the need of replenishment and intake—that is universal law nowhere more manifestly operative than in personal experience.

Our situation today, therefore, little as it may outwardly seem to do so, leads our thought straight into the realm of prayer, and that, too, by a route that should make the matter cogent. In quiet, easy days we may approach prayer speculatively, arguing our differing theories concerning it; but having myself done that aplenty, it is not my interest now. Today one needs intake to match output. If prayer means that, as the great exemplars of prayer have said it does, then let us have it somehow or other! A bright youth, fresh from the university, argues with me that prayer is theoretically irrational, but all the time he is talking I keep thinking of some hard-hitting, hard-living man, who is finding in prayer a sustaining source of power that sees him through troubled and laborious days. What I want to know is, what is that force? Never mind the name, what is that power and how does one get it?

ON BEING FIT TO LIVE WITH

Jesus came to the crisis of his life, when he knew once for all that the cross confronted him, and taking his disciples to the lovely retreat of Caesarea Philippi, under the shadow of Mount Hermon, he told them so. It was a tense and nervous time in the Master's life. He was going to Jerusalem to face the cross. Then we read that Jesus prayed. For a moment, at least, put aside theoretical skepticism about prayer and face the realistic facts. "As he was praying," we read, "the fashion of his countenance was altered." Had he too looked tense and drawn, harassed and afraid? Had his face, too, revealed his inner struggle, as he felt today's strain and foresaw tomorrow's peril? While he was praying, so Dr. Moffatt translates it, "the appearance of his face altered." Faith for fear, strength for anxiety, confidence for hesitation, inward power adequate for outward tension—that showed in his face. Theory or no theory, call it by what name we will, if that kind of experience is possible today, we need it.

In these difficult times this need is critical. Nine times out of ten, what breaks us down is an external strain plus a sense of internal inadequacy to meet it. Suppose we ask ourselves now what we are worrying about. We are worrying about the post-war world, about economic conditions, about our work, about our personal relationships, and endless other strains and problems. But press the matter more intimately home, and what each of us is really worrying about is himself and his own stamina. Many of us feel like trees in a high wind, and asked what occasions our anxiety, we naturally say, These tempests. But what we are really anxious about is our own rootage. If we knew that we had roots deep-set enough to stand tempests, our morale would not be shaken.

At this point the deepest need in us meets the deepest fact in Christianity, and if today these two could be brought together, the result might change the course of many a life. Some of us are like cisterns—we are good as far as we go; we have our uses, but we cannot count on ourselves; the sources of our supply are superficial; our reserves are limited; we cannot stand a prolonged drought. But some are like artesian wells, with resources that run deep, not at the mercy of transient circumstance. As Jesus said, "The water that I shall give him shall become in him a well of water springing up."

If such an experience of unfailing interior supply, that the great exemplars of prayer have borne witness to, is really possible, we need it, and this deep need in us corresponds with the deep resource the Christian Gospel offers: "Strengthened with might by his Spirit in the inner man." Many religious people never experience this. Christianity involves a great theology, and all of us reared in the churches have absorbed at least a smattering of that. Christianity involves a great ethic, and we have, by contagion at least, caught some of its ideals and accepted some of its obligations. Christianity involves a great fellowship, and we have in some degree assumed responsibilities for the church. Theology, ethics, church—these three make up the Christianity of multitudes. They have everything, that is, except the pith of the matter—the vital inward transforming climax of it all—God in us, a dependable resource of daily power, an unfailing well.

Asked whether we believe in God, most of us would say, Yes. But how little that affirmation sometimes means! What God do we believe in? To which some would answer, We are not materialists; we believe that the basic creative reality in the universe is Mind, not matter; and with that I, for one, would cordially agree. But is that all? To which others would say, We believe in Christ as God's revealer, and see the light of the knowledge of the Divine Glory in his face; and with that, also, I would agree. But again, Is that all? God, the creative Mind, behind and in the universe, God revealed in the supreme historic Character—is that all? Too few of us, with any accent of genuine experience, would be able to go on to the affirmation that makes the New Testament a book of triumphant living in a desperate time—God a spiritual presence in us: "Know ye not that ye are a temple of God, and that the Spirit of God dwelleth in you?" Resource, backing, power available for daily need, making us wells and not cisterns, until in sober fact, in him who strengthens us we are able for anything—that is the deepest fact in Christianity. The New Testament glories in a three-fold experience of God—God the creative Mind, God revealed in the transcendent Character, God the indwelling Spirit whose presence, as at Pentecost, is always accompanied by the promise, "Ye shall receive power."

It is commonly not weaklings but men of competent, aggressive will-power who need this experience most. Here is one who always has been adequate for life; naturally dynamic, strongly volitional, able to tackle life hard, he has been unaware of any vital lack of power. If you want anything, like a leopard, leap for it—such admirable directness of aim and effort has distinguished him. He belongs to the aggressive activists, whose very Christianity sings,

> "Awake, my soul, stretch every nerve,
> And press with vigor on!"

I never see people like that without knowing what will come some day; soon or late it will inevitably come, their confrontation of an experience where that whole method will be as inapplicable as hammering on water.

Real sorrow, for example. My friend had a lovely five-year-old daughter killed, by accident, in front of his own house, and in his own arms he carried her shattered body into the home. What does one do for one's friend in a time like that? Certainly not talk about "stretch every nerve, and press with vigor on." A great word in the English vocabulary our preaching too commonly neglects: endurance. Active vigor needed, yes, but not that alone—vigor by itself will not cover the case. We need the inner resources that make endurance possible. And that means that a man must be a well, not a cistern.

On Being Fit To Live With

So one watches people starting out in life quite adequately, handling life with active vigor, as they run, one after another, into experiences where something deeper than vigor is needed. Serious failure, for example. Some night in his lifetime everyone comes home to find a new guest there—disappointment. What he had set his heart on has gone. In such a time, when a man cries, like Beethoven with his hearing lost, "O God, give me strength to conquer myself," how futile is mere appeal to vim and vigor, like a football coach's pep-talk to his team between halves! That is an impertinence at such a time. If one is to come through difficult experiences unembittered, unspoiled, still a real person, one needs deep resources. One must be more than a cistern.

Not alone in such experiences as sorrow and failure does this need arise but in man's search for the indispensable spiritual requirements of a satisfying life—inner peace, for example, some serenity in the soul to come home to at night and go out from in the morning. Who does not need that? But no one can get inner peace by pouncing on it, by vigorously willing to have it. Peace is a margin of power around our daily need. Peace is a consciousness of springs too deep for earthly droughts to dry up. Peace is an awareness of reserves from beyond ourselves, so that our power is not so much in us as through us. Peace is the gift, not of volitional struggle, but of spiritual hospitality. Peace is a power-question. Cisterns are anxious; wells have peace. There too, man's deepest need meets Christianity's deepest fact.

There are two aspects to every strong life—rootage and fruitage, receptivity and activity, relaxation and tension, resting back and working hard. A man who cannot do the former, can never do the latter well. He who cannot rest, cannot work; he who cannot let go, cannot hold on; he who cannot find footing, cannot go forward—never! The offices of psychiatrists are littered up with folk who have mastered the techniques of activity and aggressiveness, and who are going all to pieces now because that other technique they have failed to master: they have nothing to rest back upon.

"Let my soul take refuge from the crowding turmoil of worldly thoughts beneath the shadow of Thy wings; let my heart, this sea of restless waves, find peace in Thee, O God." That was Saint Augustine's prayer. A weak man? One of history's most momentous characters, from his early struggles with himself until at last, after an immeasurably important contribution to the world, Bishop of Hippo in North Africa, he fell on sleep, while the invading barbarians were at the city's gates and the Roman Empire was tumbling down about his ears. There is no understanding such a life without such prayer. He had something to rest back upon, and many a perilous and troubled day he prayed, and the fashion of his countenance was changed.

There are two ways to learn to pray. One is to try to argue it all out first, solve all the theoretical difficulties, and then, having our questions answered and our doubts resolved, say, Now I will try to pray. I have seldom seen that method issue in profound experience. But I have often seen another kind of thing happen—folk, that is, who started with the need of backing greater than their own, the desperate need of it, and who, theory or no theory, reached out for God and found him there, some power indubitably there that they could rest back upon, so that now they face all gainsayers with a firsthand experience no speculative argument can confute. Prayer is real. "Strengthened with might by his Spirit in the inner man"—that is real!

On the Maine Coast a boy asked an old sailor, "What is the wind?" and after a long pause the old man answered, "I don't know. I can't tell you. But I know how to hoist a sail." To someone here today I am saying, Try it, will you? Endless unanswered questions yet about the wind, but still the wind is real. Hoist your sail, and see!

The kind of prayer that thus brings power always involves affirmation, positive affirmation of faith and confidence in God, putting divine strength in the center of the picture and crowding apprehensions, anxieties and fears off the edge. Who does not face hours when doubts and dismays, anxieties and apprehensions crowd up into the center of his mind? How obsessing such hours can be! And when they come something must be done about it. The Master too had such hours. Did he not cry, "Now is my soul troubled; and what shall I say?" Did he not in Gethsemane exclaim, "My soul is exceeding sorrowful, even unto death"? So, too, at Caesarea Philippi his anxieties and forebodings crowded up into the center of his thought, and then he prayed, and lo! the perspective changed. Confidence and courage marched in; the great convictions that sustained him and the great resources that supported him moved up into the center of his soul.

Real prayer like that is always more than begging; it is affirmation.

> "Though I walk through the valley of the shadow
>   of death,
> I will fear no evil; for thou art with me"—

that is prayer.

> "Therefore will not we fear, though the earth be
> removed, and though the mountains be carried
> into the midst of the sea;
> Though the waters thereof roar and be troubled,
> though the mountains shake with the swelling
> thereof . . .
> The Lord of hosts is with us; the God of Jacob
> is our refuge"—

that is prayer.

> "They that wait for the Lord shall renew their
> strength; they shall mount up with wings as eagles;
> they shall run, and not be weary; they shall walk.
> and not faint"—

that is prayer.

"I . . . am persuaded that he is able to keep that which I have committed unto him against that day"—

that is prayer. It carries up into the center of the soul convictions and reassurances that crowd out apprehensions and fears. How do folk live without that?

John Bunyan wrote *Pilgrim's Progress* in Bedford Jail. Anxieties crowded up on him—for himself, yes, but more for his family, and especially for that blind child of his whom he most dearly loved. It was his own personal experience he was describing when he wrote about Apollyon, the foul fiend, who "stradled quite over the whole breadth of the way, and said . . . prepare thy self to die, for I swear by my Infernal Den, that thou shalt go no further, here will I spill thy soul."

Yet Bunyan's soul was not spilled; no, nor countless others' souls who have known his inner secret. Prayer can be drums and bugles in one's spirit; faiths and reassurances come marching in with it to hold one's central square and drive out the saboteurs, and great convictions blow trumpets in us. All through this congregation are lives deeply in need of that.

The way the expressions of our faces change depends a great deal on the company we are in. In one group we may look dour, but let certain persons come within our view and see how our countenances light up! The Master's prayer did that for him; it introduced him to a spiritual companionship that transfigured even the way he looked. "I am not alone," he said, "the Father is with me." We can choose our interior, spiritual company— in that brief statement lies a truth that could remake our lives. Many things in the outer world we cannot choose; there we are the victims of necessity, and during these days in particular we have to live often in depressing company. But within ourselves we can choose our spiritual companionship. There we are masters of our hospitality. There we can live in a great and stimulating fellowship.

Prayer is establishing ourselves "in a sense of God's presence by continually conversing with Him." Brother Lawrence, a medieval Catholic saint, said that. Prayer is making "frequent colloquies, or short discoursings, between God and thy own soul." Jeremy Taylor, a Protestant leader of the seventeenth century, said that. This thing we are saying now is no modern thinning out of prayer, but the essence of prayer's meaning as the great souls of the church have experienced it: the maintenance of an habitual, spiritual fellowship.

We talk much today about practical Christianity. I am all for it—Christianity that gets down to hard brass tacks, that feeds the hungry, clothes the naked and works for social reformation; the Christianity of the Good Samaritan serving those of whom Jesus said, "Inasmuch as ye have done it unto one of the least of these my brethren, ye have done it unto me." Such Christianity calls for fruit on the tree; it wants practical results. But the tree's roots are practical too, critically practical, and watching modern Christians I am concerned about that aspect of the matter. Says the Psalmist,

> "He shall be like a tree, planted by the
>   streams of water,
> That bringeth forth its fruit in its season."

Many of us need that double emphasis—rootage and fruitage. Even the Master's life reached the place where all his stress on practical service would not fill the bill. Despite that he would have been long since forgotten; what saw him through was something underground, not visible to the eye, his rootage, "a tree planted by the streams of water."

This aspect of the Master's life and of our own becomes most clear to some of us as a real experience when we think of it in terms of the companionship we live in. Thank God for our friends! When the Master's face was transfigured he too was in the company of his friends. But there was more to it than that. Even when his friends failed him, and the world turned on him a forbidding face, he still had stimulating companionship within. When he was alone, he was not alone.

Such prayer as we have been talking of releases power and that phrase ought to have vivid meaning now. Turn to an old dictionary and this is what we read about "uranium"—"A rare, heavy, white metallic element . . . has no important uses." So! Uranium—no important uses! But it has now shaken the world to its foundations, because science has released its power. Such is the task of science in the physical realm—to fulfill conditions that release power; and in the realm of the spirit that is prayer's effect too.

Christian prayer is not the endeavor to get God to do what we want. Christian prayer is the endeavor to put ourselves into such relationships with God that he can do in and for and through us, what he wants. All the worst misunderstandings and perversions of prayer start with egotism—ourselves at the center, and we endeavoring to get God to do our will. But Jesus' prayer started at the other end—God first, what he wants predominant, and prayer opening up the way for the release of his purpose, giving gangway to his action and free course to his power: "Not my will, but thine, be done." Without such prayer God can never do in, and for, and through us, what he wants to do.

For such praying these present days urgently call. For action, yes—determined, courageous, tireless action—but all the more because of that, for those interior resources that only great praying can supply. Ah Christ, two things happened to your face in those trying days. First you prayed, until your face shone; and then, we read, you set your face steadfastly to go to Jerusalem.

Standing by the Best in an Evil Time

THIS is World Communion Sunday and countless Christians around the planet will meet at the Lord's Table today to express their gratitude to Christ.

> "Love so amazing, so divine,
> Demands my soul, my life, my all"—

the Lord's Supper is centered in such gratitude. It is rightly called the Eucharist, for "Eucharist" is simply the Greek word for "Thank you."

Nevertheless, there was another aspect to that last meal Jesus ate with his disciples—not alone their gratitude toward him, but his gratitude toward them. One of the most moving scenes in the Gospels, so it seems to me, is that moment in the upper room when, as Luke tells us, Jesus looked round on his disciples and said: "It is you who have stood by me through my trials." That was rather fine of him. Those first disciples had not done so well. They had continually failed to understand him and had let him down. Peter was there, soon to deny him thrice. Even at the table, Luke tells us, a contention rose among them as to who was the greatest. They were not much to be grateful for.

To be sure, this much can be said for them—they had not altogether quit. The brief years of Jesus' ministry had been difficult, opposition mounting, foes dangerously massed against him, many and powerful, and yet despite weakness and failure those few men in the upper room were still at his side. At least they had not quit, and for that much Jesus was grateful: "You who have stood by me."

This morning we try to lift that scene out of its ancient setting and reproduce it among ourselves. Of how much history is that scene the summary! Once, they say, George Washington, in the desperate days of the Revolutionary War, reviewed a fresh contingent of raw recruits from Connecticut, and, looking at their thin and tattered ranks, said, "I have great confidence in you men of Connecticut." And one of those recruits has left the record how he wept at that and clasping his musket in his arms vowed to himself that he would do his best. So often in history has a great personality with a great cause in his heart been compelled to trust such frail backers and to be grateful for their support. Long indoctrinated in the Christian gospel, we are used to the idea that we should be grateful to Christ. But that Christ is grateful to us, that he says to us, as it were, I have great confidence in you—that idea I, for one, looking at this war-blasted world, with its shocking evidence of our Christian failure, find very disturbing. To be sure, as of those first disciples this much is true of us—we have not altogether quit. Here we are in his sanctuary, wistfully, sometimes desperately, believing in him, bound to him still by faith that will not altogether let go. In a sense, we have not quit. But were Christ to thank us—"You who have stood by me through my trials" —every one of us would feel we did not deserve that.

Certainly Christ is having trials enough. That first crucifixion was hard, but these successive crucifixions—everything he stands for denied and outraged—must be worse yet. And we, his disciples, have not prevented this ghastly horror of war and its consequence. Nothing has prevented it—not all our education, our science, our statesmanship, our jurisprudence, not all the ennobling effect of our best literature, or the civilizing influence of our art and music—nothing has prevented it. But worst of all, we Christians have not prevented it. Some six hundred million of us on earth today—we have failed to stave off this catastrophe. Were Christ to condemn us as unworthy of him, we should feel the justice of that. But to be grateful to us!

Nevertheless, let us picture him today thanking us as he did his first disciples. What would it do to us to hear him out of the unseen saying to us what he said to them?

For one thing, it would surely be humbling. To those first disciples it must have been that. One can imagine what unhappy memories flashed through their minds when Jesus thanked them—James and John recalling his well deserved rebuke to them: "Ye know not what manner of spirit ye are of"; Peter recalling his Lord's stern censure—"Get thee behind me, Satan"; all of them remembering deplorable scenes, as when they tried to keep little children from coming near him, or when, slow of understanding, they faced his question: "Are you totally ignorant?" Such humiliating memories, I suspect, poured into their minds when Jesus said, "You who have stood by me."

Here is a strange fact about us all. When we face scathing condemnation from outsiders, self-defense is at once aroused, and we vigorously justify ourselves against accusation; but when, from the inside, someone whom we love gratefully praises us and assures us of all we have meant to him, we at once feel humble and begin to accuse ourselves. Were a stranger to criticize my relationships with my father, accusing me of having been a poor son to him, I should resentfully rise in self-defense. But if today out of the unseen I should hear my father himself saying, You were a good son to me, a loyal son, I would of course be melted into humility. Oh no, I would say, not half good enough, not half! and memories would rise of all the things I might have been to him, and was not.

We are a queer lot. One minute, reacting to attack from outside, we defend ourselves; the next minute, responding to gratitude from the inside, we accuse ourselves.

Just that is happening among Christians today. When bitter assaults are made, as they are made, on Christianity, the Christian church, and on us as Christians, we resent the attack and defend ourselves. When in a recent book I read this sentence: "The wholesale murder, torture, persecution and oppression we are witnessing in the middle of the twentieth century proves the complete bankruptcy of Christianity as a civilizing force," my dander rises. Hold on! I say, what do you mean, "complete bankruptcy"? The best we still have left in our western heritage came from Christianity, and mad as the world is, think what it would be if Christianity had not been here at all. And when that same writer, having utterly damned Christianity, says that only one thing can save the world, namely the law, I am indignant. If anything has broken down, I retort, the law has. The failure of law to cover our international relationships is the very gist of our catastrophe. Thus today Christianity is being passionately attacked from the outside, and passionately defended from the inside, and that gets us nowhere.

Today I prescribe another kind of medicine. Suppose that from the unseen we should hear Christ saying to us, "You who have stood by me through my trials." Is there any Christian here who would not feel the answer rising in his heart? Oh no, Lord, we would say, we have not stood by you. We have badly failed you. Look at us with the world going to hell, all obsessed as we have been with our miserable sectarianisms, creedalisms, ritualisms, still tithing mint, anise and cummin, and neglecting the weightier matters of the law. We have not stood by you. We Christians and the whole Christian church profoundly need to be converted. Antichrist has whipped us, because we have put so many lesser, trivial things in place of genuine loyalty to you. In the very heart of Europe, where Christianity has had its long chance, some six million of your own people brutally slain in cold blood! Do not thank us for standing by you!

Friends, that mood—not defensive self-justification, but humility—is the healthy one for us Christians to be in. We call on the wicked world to repent, but we Christians ourselves had better repent. And such penitence does not come from vehement self-defense against outside attack. It comes from the thought of Christ himself, after all our failures still trying to be grateful to us, if only because we have not altogether quit. Let us take that to ourselves today, one by one! I find it disturbing. If I could, I would run away from it—that picture of Christ trying to say to me, "It is you who have stood by me through my trials." Alas! what failures—personal failures, world failures—that conjures up.

Nevertheless, to say that is not the whole story. This word of Jesus awakens another response; not humbling only, it is dignifying too. Those first disciples must have felt that. Unworthy to have it said of them—yes—but still, if only it were a little true, it was the finest thing that could be said of them. I wonder if those words of Jesus did not become a slogan oft repeated in their thinking in the after years, when the Christian cause was hard bestead, the going difficult, on days when life sagged down and gloom closed in—"It is you who have stood by me through my trials."

What is it that gives dignity to life, lifts it out of mediocrity, saves it from futility and insignificance and makes it in the long run worth living? To get one's eye on the best, even in a bad time, and to stand by that! We are not much as individuals; we can terribly despise ourselves; but there is something that can give even our small lives dignity and significance. To have seen the best in our time, and to have stood by it—that does elevate even the humblest life to dignity and worth.

Let no one push this off as though it were an ideal, visionary matter of being spiritually noble and all that. It is a matter of being fundamentally a worth-while human being, healthy and strong, with a life that is at all worth living. Dr. Jung, the pioneer psychiatrist, quotes one of his patients as saying: "If only I knew that my life had some meaning and purpose, then there would be no silly story about my nerves!" Just so! That sums up countless cases, all knocked to pieces because life has been futile, with no meaning and dignity in it. And the secret of dignity in life is the consciousness that with all our failures

there is some best, some Christ, by whom and for whom we
have stood in our time.

Say if we will that as individuals we are futile and insignificant,
we do not need to be that. Sir Alfred Zimmern, one of our leading
experts in international affairs at Oxford University, was one
day walking in the gardens there with Basil Mathews when
Mathews asked him, "What, in your opinion, is the greatest
obstacle between us and the building of enduring world peace?"
And Sir Alfred's unhesitating answer was, "The small-scale
individual." So that's the ultimate trouble—the small-scale
individual who in an era terrific in its chaos, ominous in its
perils, immense in its opportunities, gets no vision of the great
matters, of the Christ in our time, and does not stand by *that*.
This is the trouble! And this trouble is not only the curse of the
world, but the curse of the individual too. For think what could
happen to that small-scale individual, if, like those first fishermen from Galilee, who were small-scale individuals to start
with, if ever there were any, he should rise to the place where
Christ could say, even though it took divine mercy to see it,
"You who have stood by me."

This plea to the small-scale individual is critically urgent
now. Multitudes, finding themselves in this mess of a world,
respond to it by being a mess themselves. But others, often
fishermen from Galilee, men and women, that is, who might
easily be small-scale individuals, make another response. They
see the necessity of the best because the worst is so bad; they
catch a fresh vision of the Christ because Antichrist is so intolerable. It is such who across the centuries when times were
evil have preserved and furthered, in every realm, the faiths
and hopes that still sustain mankind. It was their glory that
some saving excellence could say to them, "You who have stood
by me."

As one grows older one feels the meaning of this more and
more. So many things one has cared about and worked for pass
away. But if in the end some best hope, some princely excellence

of his era, hard bestead but to which the future belongs, could say to him, though he deserved it but a little, "You who have stood by me,"—that would make everything worth while.

So Bonaro Overstreet put it:

"You say the little efforts that I make
will do no good:
they never will prevail
to tip the hovering scale
where justice hangs in balance.
      I don't think
I ever thought they would.
But I am prejudiced beyond debate
in favor of my right to choose which side
shall feel the stubborn ounces of my weight."

World Communion Sunday ought to mean this to us as Christians. If some one says that he is fed up with contemporary Christianity, its divisions, its theological hair-splitting, its dry-as-dust conventionality and all the rest—I am too, disgusted with it and ashamed. What difference do most of the things Christians split up about matter in a world like this, with Christ and Antichrist at loggerheads and the fate of all mankind in the balance? You are right to be disgusted with it, but not with Christ—not with his master faiths and principles of life. To be a Christian is to stand by Christ. Get that basic, central matter clear, for Christ towers up today more relevant to our need, more certainly the hope of the future, than I for one have ever seen him. I want some young man or woman here today to make a decision, so that thirty, forty years from now he too can hear the Christ, humbling him, yet dignifying him, too: "You who have stood by me."

· Humbling and dignifying this word of Jesus is, but it is challenging too. Let us face that before we stop. In days like these, someone has got to stand by the great spiritual heritage that has come down to us in Christ. None of us really wants that lost out of the world. We all of us are pensioners on it. The best in our lives, our homes, our societies has come from it.

We say that Christianity has been here two thousand years, as though that were a long time, but it isn't. When one thinks what kind of world this is, when beneath the thin veneer of civilization one sees the unredeemed brutality in human nature, and when one considers the contrasting heights of life and character, personal and social, to which Christ calls us, two thousand years are not long. We are still, as it were, in the infancy of Christianity, its message still appearing to most of the world incredibly too good to be true, too difficult to be tried.

We are not the first generation to be discouraged by the contemporary scene. Victor Hugo reminds us that we now think of the sixteenth century as one of history's main turning points, with the Protestant Reformation and all the rest, but that Erasmus, who lived then, called it "the excrement of the ages"; that we see in the seventeenth century thrilling discovery and adventure, opening up the whole new world, but that Bossuet, in the thick of it, called it "a wicked and paltry age"; that to us the eighteenth century presents a stirring scene of political liberation, with the French and American Revolutions and the like, but that even Rousseau in a disheartened hour described it as "This great rottenness amidst which we live." So in the sixteenth, seventeenth and eighteenth centuries the people who really fooled themselves were the skeptics, the cynics, while those who saw the possibilities and with a faith that moved mountains believed in them were realistically right. Surely, in this regard, history can repeat itself in our century, if we only stand by the best.

In that upper room it was a gamble when those first disciples stood by Christ. How little they had to go on, with the whole world against him! But we know now that they were right. Caesar and the whole Roman Empire were as ephemeral as a skyrocket compared with him. And if in our day, in personal character, in faith and loyalty, we join those first disciples, we shall be right. Whether or not you actually sit at any church's communion table this Sunday, may the day have this meaning in your experience—that you do join them, that you bet your life as they did theirs that when all the Romes have fallen Christ will still be here.

It is not generals alone, but privates, who get the Victoria Cross and the Congressional Medal, and this is the Victoria Cross, the Congressional Medal of Christian life—to deserve even a little: "It is you who have stood by me through my trials."

On Worshiping Things We Manufacture

IN THE Book of Micah, as Dr. Moffatt translates it, God
says something through his prophet that he might well
say to us: "You must no longer worship things you manufacture." To be sure, those words concern, not scientific inventions, but idolatrous images, but while the form of the situation
has changed, the substance of the truth is still the same. Through
this ghastly catastrophe that afflicts mankind today, God is saying to us, if we would only hear him: "You must no longer
worship things you manufacture."

We modern folk have stood before the works of our inventive genius and our skillful hands with boundless admiration,
trusting them to build for us a better earth. A hundred years
ago the scientific mastery of the world was just beginning, the
first trains running from New York to cities like Albany and
Boston, no elevators or refrigerators, no electric lights, no vic-
trolas, radios, telephones, automobiles, or airplanes; yes, no
T.N.T., no submarines, no atom bombs, no possibility of global
war. For three generations, with absorbed attention man has
been inventing and producing this amazing paraphernalia of
our modern world, before whose consequence we elders still
stand half incredulous. During the war at my alma mater, Col-
gate University, where we conducted courses for airmen, a
young man, ten minutes late for registration at the term's beginning, excused himself when the officer rebuked him. "I am
sorry to be late, sir," he said, "but yesterday I was in Africa."

We could not have lived through such a time without glorying in the things we manufacture, but now we confront a sober-
ing situation. "Everybody," wrote Robert Louis Stevenson, "soon
or late sits down to a banquet of consequences." There we are
now, facing a momentous and terrifying fact about our modern

world; namely, that in this amazing work of our hands we have created the instruments by which mankind can destroy itself.

To feel the full force of that we ought to attend church under more precarious conditions, instead of sitting so safely in our pews. One who worshiped with Dr. Weatherhead's City Temple congregation in London during the war wrote this: "A bomb passed immediately overhead with a terrific roar yesterday morning, and I thought we were all for it. The nervous tension is so great that it is impossible to concentrate—one is just holding one's breath all the time . . . Going to church yesterday morning was one of the hardest things I have ever done in my life, and I was a nervous wreck for the rest of the day." If we could have shared such experience, which one way or another millions have endured, the words of the prophet would sound in our ears with inescapable urgency: "You must no longer worship things you manufacture."

Whatever the solution of our human problem, it lies not in these material instruments we use but in the spirit of man who uses them, in his character, in the moral aims he is devoted to, in the God of justice and good will he believes in and serves. Not in our mastery of the material realm but in the spiritual realm's mastery of us lies the solution of our appalling problem. If someone calls that a platitude, I protest. The great mass of mankind does not today believe that at all. Look at them and see! Do men really believe that the only solution of the human problem is spiritual? Do they act as if they did? Upon the contrary, millions in this country—can it be that there are none such here today?—treat the spiritual as secondary, as at best a decorative addition to life; they do not put it first; they do not see that the only way out from our catastrophe lies there; they push even such religion as they have to the side lines as though it did not apply to the whole world's critical need; their eyes are still on man's mastery of the material, and on the new inventions that will emerge after the war. So, unchastened by the world's tragedy, we go on with the same old idolatry. To be rid of that is one of the most urgent problems of our time.

In making this real to ourselves, consider first that we moderns had better give up any proud self-complacency about our boasted scientific civilization and become humble and penitent concerning it. Up to date we are not a success. Up to date our modern civilization is a frightening failure.

The generation in which I grew up, commonly believing in automatic and inevitable progress, was characterized by an optimistic pride never before equaled in history. Samuel Butler, a typical member of that old generation wrote: "Give the world time, an infinite number of epochs, and according to its past and present system, like the coming tide each epoch will advance on each, but so slowly that it can hardly be traced, man's body becoming finer to bear his finer mind, till man becomes not only an angel but an archangel." Well, do you see any signs of man's becoming an archangel? Samuel Butler was a militant atheist, hoping for all this heavenly consequence on earth as the result of material forces only, mastered by man's intelligent control. What a fool's paradise that was!

Today another kind of voice speaks, Winston Churchill, for example, writing prophetically in 1924: "Nations who believe their life is at stake will not be restrained from using any means to secure their existence. . . . among the means which will next time be at their disposal will be agencies and processes of destruction wholesale, unlimited, and perhaps, once launched, uncontrollable. Mankind has never been in this position before. Without having improved appreciably in virtue or enjoying wiser guidance, it has got into its hands for the first time the tools by which it can unfailingly accomplish its own extermination." So!

For many years I have tried to preach the gospel of Christ, but never with such a sense of urgency as now. The issues which Christ raises in this modern world are not secondary, decorative, peripheral, but central, a matter of life and death. No longer can anyone who sees the truth, push Christ's gospel off as merely an individual matter of saving our own souls. The world's affairs, as well, are at stake. Here we are, with our boasted scientific civilization, as H. G. Wells pictures us, like "children in a nursery," into whose hands science has put poisoned razor blades, bombs, corrosive fluids and all the rest, while we have no nurse to intervene, save humanity's poor wisdom. The cure does not lie in more scientific power to produce more poisoned razor blades, bombs and corrosive fluids; the salvation lies in another realm altogether that the great mass of mankind rejects, neglects, treats as secondary, and pushes to the side lines of its thought and its devotion.

Yet, these tremendous powers that science gives us are going to fall under somebody's control. If they are dominated by the unredeemed devil in man, we are done for! If they were used by men and women in whom the spirit of Christ were in control, what could not be done on earth! That issue is the most critical mankind ever faced.

This situation puts a fresh and serious meaning into the word "sin." During the war and during this year of disillusioning aftermath, we have faced the fact that the decencies of human life, the spiritual qualities that redeem life from brutality, and give to man his moral dignity and worth, can turn out to be a very thin veneer, and close beneath the surface the old savage, more beastly than the beasts. Moreover, in our day, the old savage is no longer merely the old savage, but is now the primitive barbarian armed with the instruments of modern science. When one thinks of sin today that fact moves up into the center of the picture, no petty breaches of moral custom such as too often the church has wasted its time upon, but this huge matter, that something abysmally wrong, an unredeemed savagery in the heart of man, can arm itself with the murderous instruments of modern science, and wreck the world. That is sin, giving an exhibition of itself that I should suppose the stoutest heart would be appalled by.

Seeing sin thus, as the world's catastrophe presents it, one central message becomes indispensable. We cannot be saved from this sin by anything we make; this sin flourishes on what we make; our salvation from this can come only from the recognition of something we did not make, that was before us and will be after us, the Eternal, that made us. Put the matter impersonally at first, if you will, and call this superior element the moral law. If we made that, we can change it. We can put right for wrong, and wrong for right. But what if we did not make it? What if the moral law was here first, an eternal right and an eternal wrong? What if cruelty, tyranny, the denial of liberty, hatred, and the lust for selfish power, are wrong, not because we make it so, but because Eternal God made it so? Then our salvation lies in acknowledging that, being obedient to that.

Before it is too late we had better come back to such great religion. We are Frankensteins, who have created a technological civilization that in the hands of sin can literally exterminate us. If someone says that I am putting the matter in gloomy terms, too unrelieved, and that there are hopeful elements in the situation, I answer, To be sure, but what are the hopeful elements? Hitler and Niemoeller once confronted each other, Hitler openly glorying in being a ruthless savage, armed with the instruments of modern science, and Niemoeller still clinging to that other realm of superior spiritual truth and reality, to which his primary loyalty was due. And though prison was the price of it, Niemoeller said to Hitler, "God is my Fuehrer!" Whatever hopeful elements there are in human society today are of that quality—the Eternal above us, his law sovereign over us, his righteousness not something we make but that he made, his grace not our creation but his gift.

Henry Adams, author of the book, *The Education of Henry Adams*, that a few years ago had great vogue, wrote in 1900 a letter from Paris, saying that every afternoon he went to the World Exposition there and prayed to the dynamo. He had, he said, nothing else left to worship and the dynamo had emerged as the last word in the modern world, with power to do magical things for man. "Why," he wrote, "shouldn't the dynamo be worthy of worship?" That is what modern man as a whole has said, but the answer to that seems obvious enough today. Millions going to the ends of the earth to fight and die in a global war—if we are going to stop the ever recurrent repetition of that, we must worship something else besides the dynamo. Give to Christ even a little of the devotion we have given to the things we manufacture and we might be saved.

With this in mind, turn now to some practical facts about our situation that light up this urgent truth. The things we manufacture are the most easily transmissible elements in human life; they spread like wildfire. Invent a railroad here, and railroads will soon be everywhere. Start radio here and it will shortly encompass the globe. Invent one successful airplane and every land will soon hear the hum of motors in the sky. Japan woke up late to modern scientific inventions but within a generation Japan had absorbed and made her own all the things we manufacture. This modern technological civilization, with its stupendous powers for good or evil, will be increasingly a world-wide affair. But the great faiths, the spiritual loyalties to those high ends that mean man's peace and brotherhood, do not spread so fast; they lag behind. A man of realistic mind, therefore, who does not wish to live in a fool's paradise, confronts now a whole world, increasingly equipped with gigantic aggregations of destructive power, with the saying of Alfred the Great still true: "Power is never a good unless he be good that has it."

You will not suppose that I underestimate the immeasurable service that modern science has rendered us. Thank God for science! But that grateful, optimistic view of it in terms of its marvelous achievements for good, is not enough today. In the large view, science is not solving but creating our problem, and above all, our world problem, where its stupendous powers, falling under the control of unredeemed spirits, ominously threaten us. The message which today the world critically needs is this: we have modern science on our hands; we cannot escape it; it is here to stay and grow and put ever wider areas of power under our control; its mastery of cosmic forces increases daily our capacity to lift or to destroy mankind, and spreads with frightening rapidity to all races and nations; unless great ethical religion can catch up with all this new power, begetting in mankind's soul devotion to moral aims that put righteousness and decency, justice and brotherhood first, our science will be used to destroy us.

Our modern peril comes even more intimately home to us when we see that the inventions of science are not only the most swiftly transmissible factors in our life, from nation to nation, but from generation to generation. It is not difficult for parents to hand down to children the things we manufacture; the new generation takes to them like ducks to water. But not so simple is it to hand down to our sons and daughters a rich spiritual culture, the great heritage of Christ's faith and ethics, and we are not doing well at that. Many families in America are paying little heed to that, and in our schools that is commonly not even permitted.

I am pleading today with us who are here to start where we are, with our lives, with our families, with our churches. We can help at least a little. If this situation we face—science arming all races and nations and each successive generation with new, tremendous instruments of power, while man's saving faiths, his spiritual wisdom, and his loyalty to moral aims lag far behind—does not arouse and persuade us, no pulpit can do it.

Have you a grandchild? Can you look at him without thinking of this? The kind of world he is going to live in depends on the spiritual quality that will use the powers his generation will control, powers so immense that we cannot now imagine them. I talked with a man the other day who knows from the inside what is going on in some of our laboratories. He was not exultant. He was sober and fearful. The new powers coming into man's hands, he said, are appalling. It's a race between education and catastrophe, we used to say. It's more than that; it is a race now between Christ's principles of life and chaos.

To be sure, Christ lived long ago; he knew nothing about the things we manufacture; but if because of that we elide him from our modern world we are making the mistake of our lives. Put our scientific inventiveness under the control of his spirit and such a future beckons mankind as no dreams of ours can adequately picture. But let them run loose, fall into barbarian hands, become the tools of unredeemed human nature, and heaven have mercy on our grandchildren!

Over the grave of Colonel Patterson who fell in battle in Italy, the chaplain put as an epitaph words that had been familiar on the Colonel's lips. At first he used them as a description of effective military strategy but then, seeing deeper meaning in them, he took them as his philosophy of life: "Always take the high ground and the enemy will flee." Taking the high ground, giving ourselves with a faith and loyalty no situation can discourage and no disappointment defeat to putting first the Kingdom of God and his righteousness—that is desperately needed in our nations and homes and personal lives.

On the air, when commentators from abroad have finished their narration of the news, we commonly hear the parting sentence: I return you to New York. So I say now: I return you to New York, and of all places in the world where it is easy to worship things we manufacture and forget the Christ we ought to devote them to, New York is as tempting as any. Yet look at New York and see if that question of the Master is not urgent and critical here, concerning all the interests we treasure most: What shall it profit to gain the whole world and lose the soul?

The Constructive Use of Fear

FEAR is one of the most powerful emotions in human experience and everyone feels its pressure now. A sober, realistic fear haunts all mankind, a serious foreboding not to be exorcised like a demon and banished from our souls. More than once I have preached about fear, but always, I discover, in terms of surmounting and getting rid of it. Some psychopathic dreads and terrors we should get rid of. In this congregation there must be many an abnormal anxiety, the symptom of a sick soul, which the kind of insight wise psychiatry can give and the strength a vital Christian faith can furnish could overcome. But the fear that haunts mankind now, far from being the symptom of a sick soul is the insight of a realistic mind. We should be fools were we not afraid. As Angelo Patri has said, "Education consists in being afraid at the right time."

One of Aesop's fables describes a lion and a goat quarreling at a water-hole as to which should drink first. There was plenty of room for them to drink together, but none the less they quarreled about precedence and were preparing to fight it out when, looking up, they saw the vultures wheeling low above them, waiting for the battle and its aftermath. So, says the fable, they decided to drink together. Certainly the vultures are flying low over the world today; they have picked the bones of previous civilizations that fought it out, and they may pick ours yet. Only a fool feels no fear.

This fear we speak of, therefore, well justified and not to be dismissed, we must handle one way or another. Something must and will be done with it for good or evil. What if it could be harnessed to great ends? What if instead of a curse it could become a blessing?

[125]

The Bible plainly teaches fear's twofold meaning. Sometimes in the Bible fear is an intruder to be driven out, an enemy to be overcome.

> "The Lord is my light and my salvation;
> Whom shall I fear?"

cries the psalmist; and from Jesus saying, "Fear not," to John's Epistle, saying, "Perfect love casteth out fear," the New Testament proclaims a faith that conquers anxiety and fright. The Bible, however, contains another message also. "The fear of the Lord is the beginning of wisdom," says the Old Testament; and Dr. Goodspeed rightly translates Paul's message to the Romans: "You ought not to feel proud; you ought to be afraid." So there is a place in life for fear well used. In an era like our own, Jeremiah heard God say of his people: "I will put my fear in their hearts, that they may not depart from me."

That is common sense. Only this last week General MacArthur appealed to it: "Another war may blast mankind to perdition, but still we hesitate, still we cannot, despite the yawning abyss at our very feet, unshackle ourselves from the past." Such is our situation, with the question rising, Are we, or are we not, going to make a constructive use of fear?

Consider, to start with, the way we often take for granted and treat lightly the supreme values in our lives until some shocking day we face the danger of their loss. The Prodigal Son in Jesus' parable is typical of us all. Son of a good home, he took for granted respectability, social status, economic security, family love. Were not such values his heritage? He assumed them as inherently his possessions. And then in the Far Country one dreadful day he faced the fact that he could lose them, was losing them. No wise counselor would have told that scared youth to banish fear; his fear was healthy, valid, intelligent, and the push and pressure of it sent him home.

Fear, therefore, can be the great turning point in a man's

life. In how many homes has this not happened? We felt secure, the love of wife or husband, the love of children, the peaceful harbor of a happy family from which to sail and to which to return—we loved it and took it for granted; and so, secure, we became careless, the conditions of a true home neglected, minor infidelity growing toward major betrayal, the rift in the lute left unmended, the secret hurt unallayed, until some day the hidden peril became outspoken and explicit. The home could be lost—that fact stared us in the face. All the priceless values there, that really were our heart's chief treasure, might go up in smoke. Many a family has to go through that frightening experience before it comes to its true self. As a Scotchman once said, it is sometimes true that the Kingdom of God is not for the well-meaning but for the desperate.

The Bible says that God is in such fear. Our modern Christianity, much too sentimental, when asked where we find God, has commonly said, We find him in all that is lovely and beautiful, like Wordsworth, in nature, feeling a presence that disturbs us "with the joy of elevated thoughts." Wherever love is, and goodness and beauty—there is God. I agree. I have come out from Carnegie Hall after hearing the Ninth Symphony gloriously rendered, sure that in a world where such resplendent beauty is, God must be.

That, however, is not the whole story. John Bunyan once said that in his unregenerate days he used to walk across Bedford Green and fairly smell the sulphurous fumes coming up through the grass roots from the hell he feared. That old theology has gone but in days like these one sometimes does feel as though one walked across the thin crust of a hell into which we verily might plunge, we and our children and all the choicest values we have cherished. How can anyone escape that dread? And is it not God, as Jeremiah said, who is putting his fear into our hearts? Not simply in the loveliness of springtime and the spell of glorious music do we meet him but in those great moral arbitraments of history when men, nations and civilizations confront the loss of the values they hold dear.

Well, we cannot take our civilization for granted any more! Let's not fool ourselves—we can lose it! One more war, armed with atomic energy, and what will be left of civilization? If someone says such fear can be shattering, I say, Yes! but such fear can be constructive too, not panic, but positively turning our tame, moderate, halfhearted faith into a flaming loyalty to the spiritual values that more vividly than ever before we perceive must not be lost.

Some of the greatest days in history have come when evils faced mankind, so monstrous that all decent folk feared them, and when the best of men rose up, their deep instincts of revolt aroused, to say, This is intolerable, better die than endure it! So men feared ignorance, and revolted against it to seek knowledge, though the price was heavy for the pioneers. So men feared tyranny, and rebelling against it sought liberty and democracy at all costs. So the early Christians feared paganism—

> "On that hard Pagan world disgust
> And secret loathing fell"—

and revolting against it sought the Christian way of life, come what might to them. Today, we critically need this spirit—a sober, indignant, moving recognition of the fact that in our personal and social life there is let loose a monstrous paganism we had better fear, and against which our deep instincts of revolt had better be aroused. So may God make the fear of the Lord now the beginning of wisdom!

Consider further how great a blessing a healthy fear can be in breaking down our cheap optimism and our silly trust in superficial reliances. Ever since evolution was accepted in biology man's wishful thinking has been tempted to carry over its application to all man's social life, and to deduce from it the doctrine of inevitable, automatic progress. Despite the protests of the wise, the idea has captured the imagination of the populace that willy-nilly we are on an ascending road, era by era getting better and better. But, look at the world! Inevitable, automatic progress is nonsense. As Professor Radhakrishnan recently said, the more we know the worse we behave.

Alfred Noyes, in his poem, "Watchers of the Sky," describes Galileo showing his new telescope to the senators of Florence and the old men, wagging their white beards, say to one another,

> "This glass will give us great advantages
> In time of war."

So, presented by science with a gift that could expand the mind and spirit of the race, those old men thought first of "great advantages in time of war," and Alfred Noyes exclaims:

> "O God of love,
> Even amidst their wonder at thy world,
> Dazed with new beauty, gifted with new powers,
> These old men dreamed of blood."

What, then, would Noyes say now, when the long dream of science has been fulfilled—the atom split—such energy available for mankind's service as could usher in unprecedented plenty, and still, contemplating it, the old men dream of blood.

The doctrine of automatic, inevitable progress is sheer nonsense. As a student in the Seminary years ago I recall one of our professors saying, "Beware how you baptize evolution with optimism." Just so! New knowledge, yes; new power, yes; new possibilities, yes; but still from worse to worse we can plunge on if we lack new character to handle it. Paul's words are true for us, with all our boasted modern science: "You ought not to feel proud; you ought to be afraid."

Well, we are! No question is much more important now than what we are going to do with fear. It can be a shattering emotion, confusing judgment, paralyzing effort, displacing faith with cynicism and hope with dismay. All through this congregation are people in whom the world's haunting fear may have such consequence, and what we are saying is that fear need not be so misused.

Behind every great achievement of mankind stands a fear. With our besetting sentimentalism we interpret schools, for example, solely in terms of man's aspiration. Schools, we say, spring from man's aspiration after learning. True enough! Aspiration was the pull, but there was a push too—fear of illiteracy and ignorance. Is our medical science the result of aspiration only? No, medical science comes from fear too, of dread diseases that for ages have struck terror into human hearts. Fear can be constructively used; it lies behind every great achievement of mankind. As Ralph Waldo Emerson said, "Fear is an instructor of great sagacity and the herald of all revolutions."

It had better be the herald of a revolution now, and that revolution must begin first of all inside people one by one. The world is not automatically getting better and it never will. "A regenerated society can only be composed of regenerated men," said Lord Eustace Percy. "To expect a change in human nature may be an act of faith; but to expect a change in human society without it is an act of lunacy." What an era this might turn out to be if we would have it so! Our posterity might see it as one of history's great ages, not despite the fact that it is dreadful but because it is dreadful, so dire that we were aroused personally and publicly to seek those things that belong unto our peace. So may God make in each of us the fear of the Lord the beginning of wisdom.

Follow our truth further and see that fear can arouse us to a fresh devotion on behalf of great social causes. Maybe we ought to serve great social causes from pure, idealistic motives only, waking up every morning thinking of what good we can do the world, but alas! we are not like that. Especially if everything is going well, we are not. Says Shakespeare in Macbeth:

> ". . . security
> Is mortals' chiefest enemy."

We dislike facing that fact. We love security. With all my heart I believe in our social security measures. And yet as I know my own selfishness I see what a self-centered, undedicated life security can beget. Then security vanishes, and fear comes, and democracy and liberty and civilization and Christianity are in danger; and what pure, idealistic motives could not do, fear does—wakes us up, makes us care as we never cared before about what happens to our society.

For that use of fear we are pleading now. Let us make it specific! We fear Russia. We do not want to, but we do, and the evil results of that fear are rampant. Fear begets panic, and many are growing jittery; fear begets hatred, and hatred of Russia grows; fear begets violence, and some, even so soon, talk of war with Russia. If we let fear of Russia take such courses we shall repeat an age-old disaster, that fear brings to pass what it fears.

Now fear of Russia cannot be lightly dismissed. Soviet Russia's social organization violates some of the most dearly prized values of our American democracy. In this next generation we do face a colossal competition between two deeply divergent social systems—Soviet communism and our type of democracy. But all the more because we see and feel this, may God help us now to make a constructive use of our fear—not panic, not hatred, not war, but a fresh dedication of ourselves to make our own democracy so effective in what it does for all the people that it will prove its superior ability to meet man's needs.

The ultimate criterion that will decide the issue between Soviet communism and American democracy is which of the two in the long run does the more for the common man. Soviet communism, with all its ruthless cruelty and its denial of personal liberty, has done a lot for the common man in Russia who never has known what liberty in our sense means. In World War I the Russians fought inefficiently; in World War II they fought magnificently; and one reason for the difference, as everybody knows, is that under the czars the common man had little to fight for, but under the Soviet regime he had gained such a degree of dignity, of literacy, of economic welfare and hope that he was willing to die for his cause. Which, now, in the long run, will do more for the common man—Soviet communism, or our type of democracy? That is the towering question, on which the issue in the end depends.

"Capitalism is on trial, and on the issue of this trial may depend the whole future of western civilization." The Dean of the Graduate School of Business Administration at Harvard said that. He is right! All social systems are on trial—notably Russian communism and capitalistic democracy—and war will not settle the issue; the issue will be determined in the end by which social system does the more for the common man. Were I talking to Russians I could say some damning things about their system, but I am talking to Americans, and this issue comes home to us here, with our slums, our appalling masses of the under-privileged, our embittered minorities, our racial discrimination. Recently in New York City we have had a public revelation of slum conditions such that ever since I have been haunted by the exclamation of an Englishman: "What's the use of living in an empire on which the sun never sets, if one has to live in an alley on which the sun never rises?" If we are going successfully to compete with Russian communism we must meet it where the real issue is: which opens the wider door of hope to the plain people?

Sometimes when I am tired I am glad that I will not be in the thick of this next generation's tremendous battle, but in better hours I envy you young men and women of America. It is going to be a great struggle, but never forget where the heart of the struggle lies. The plain people—how well off are they, and where are they better off, in Russia or here? That is the issue. So may God help us to make the fear of the Lord the beginning of wisdom.

Here, then, is the conclusion of the matter. The constructive use of fear ought to lead us Christians to see afresh the meaning and necessity of Christ. Sum up this horrid scene that rightly frightens us, and is not the essence of it Antichrist? Many of you here would say, as I do, that all my life I have believed in Christ. Yet often faith in him has been tame, mild, moderate, one of the lovely side lines of our lives, like music. But how can a Christian now look at this world, fearful in its possibilities when Antichrist assumes control, and not feel his faith in Christ burning with a fiercer flame?

Do we think the saints and prophets have believed in Christ, as they have, solely because of idealistic love for the highest when they saw it? Indeed not! They faced Christ in the light of the alternatives. They saw paganism, as we have seen it in our time, and were afraid. They looked into the hell that utter Christlessness involves, and from that they turned, not simply in aspiration but in desperation, to seek the saviorhood he offers.

I just quoted Emerson about fear as an instructor of great sagacity and the herald of all revolutions. But Emerson said something else about fear: "He is a carrion crow, and though you see not well what he hovers for, there is death somewhere . . . That obscene bird is not there for nothing. He indicates great wrongs which must be revised." He does indeed! And who will right those wrongs, give mankind abundant life, make personality inwardly rich, crown our societies with brotherhood and peace, except the Christ and what he stands for? This would be a constructive use of fear, if it should lead us personally and publicly to seek his way of life—the fear of the Lord the beginning of wisdom.

On Catching the Wrong Bus

RECENTLY the newspapers carried the story of a man who boarded a bus with the full intention and desire of going to Detroit, but when at the end of a long trip he alighted at the destination, he found himself, not in Detroit, but in Kansas City. He had caught the wrong bus. Something like that goes on habitually in human life. People on the whole desire good things—happiness, fine family life, competence in their work, the respect of their friends, an honorable old age. Nothing is more common in our consciously held desires and intentions than such good goals, but after a long trip, how many, alighting at the destination, find themselves somewhere else altogether!

That man who started for Detroit and landed in Kansas City would not at first believe it. Stepping from the bus, he asked for Woodward Avenue, and, told there was no Woodward Avenue, he was indignant. He knew his Detroit; there was a Woodward Avenue; and protesting against inhospitable failure to direct him, it was some time before he could face the fact that despite the clarity of his desire and his intention, it was not Detroit. He had caught the wrong bus.

The Prodigal Son did not start out for a swine pasture. His desire was centered on happiness, freedom, independence, adventure—good goals, that he could justify to himself, his family and friends. Such was the admirable destination he proposed for himself and started out for, but alas! the means he chose landed him somewhere else altogether.

Life is full of this experience. These charming young couples one marries week after week all desire lovely families, and, reading their hearts in their eyes, one sees the fair dreams they cherish of the homes they plan, and of the children they hope for. But as the decades pass the minister sees so many marriages he celebrates start for Utopia, and end in Reno, that he finds himself at the marriage service offering a homely prayer that no one hears: God grant they may catch the right bus!

This truth that the destination we reach depends not on our ideals alone but on the bus we catch, is personally critical. For the most part we do desire good things: happy homes, respectable characters, an honorable standing in our fellows' eyes, useful lives not untouched by the spirit of Christ's unselfishness, and, if God wills, an old age unashamed. Say your worst about us, we have fine desires for good destinations. But often we let it go at that, contenting ourselves with these unimpeachable ideals that we think represent our real selves, whereas the critical question rises: Are we on the road that leads where we want to go, now, this morning, in our immediate, practical habits and choices? Are we on the right bus?

Never before in history, for example, did more people than now desire a great good thing, a world organized for peace and free from the curse of war. That destination we all want to reach, but multitudes, sharing that desire, are not facing the other issue—the road that leads to it, the cost of it in the surrender of old ideas of national sovereignty and old practices of imperialistic exploitation, the new outlooks required, the rethinking of our economic life, the profound moral regeneration which alone can make it possible. More than anything else I dread living to see this generation, so desperately wanting a world brotherhood of peoples, landing somewhere else altogether because it took the wrong bus.

In one of his most familiar sayings Jesus summed this matter up. We commonly think of Jesus as presenting us with the high ideals we ought to set our hearts upon, but he did not forget this other matter. "Narrow is the gate, and straitened the way, that leadeth unto life, and few are they that find it." That's it! To desire life, full, abundant, happy, free—when Jesus talks about that goal, saying, "I came that they may have life, and may have it abundantly," we find it easy to desire, but are we so willing to face the road that leads to it? "Narrow is the gate, and straitened the way, that leadeth unto life."

For one thing, in this saying of Jesus we confront the serious implications of a law-abiding universe. It is one thing to desire a great goal; it is another thing to fulfill the conditions of reaching it, and the conditions must be fulfilled. By no trick or magic can we reach the right place on the wrong bus—not in God's world!

Despite our boasted science multitudes still believe in magic, something for nothing, great ends reached without meeting the conditions. They know that is not true in the physical world, but in the spiritual realm they still think they can get away with it. At this point the Christian preacher faces a baffling problem. What can the preacher do on Sunday except present great ideas about life, high ideals for life, deep resources in life, Christ exalted as the one toward whose perfection we should strive? And if the preacher does it well there is response; we do consent to the grandeur and nobility of such ideals. But then look at the buses we get on that do not lead that way at all!

Forgive me, then, for speaking about this simple, practical, close-at-home matter today. I am tired of saying in general that as Christians our high ideal is to be Christlike, and having everyone agree, but then seeing what often comes of it, that while folk may choose that ideal as the end they seek, the means which alone can lead to it they do not choose; the disciplines, the spiritual companionships, the daily habits, the practical methods of life that alone make Christlikeness possible they do not make their own. What is the use of their idealism therefore? It is not the ideal of getting to Detroit that gets you there, but the right bus. I shall be content to preach this sermon if just one person here, checking the bus he is on, discovers that it is not going to the place he wants to land in, and changes to another.

From its first founding I have been interested in Alcoholics Anonymous, an amazing organization of men and women, all of whom were once hopeless slaves of drink and who now, re-covered to sobriety and self-control, are banded together to help their fellow victims. As one sees them, splendid, admirable people, one knows that they never set out for that dreadful place they landed in. They had fine ideals, good intentions for happy, respected, useful lives and families, and one often wonders how they ever expected to get to the place they wanted to be, on the bus they chose to travel on.

Do not misunderstand me to be belittling the importance of fine ideals. They are important. A lecturer recently, with an engagement to speak in a certain city arrived on a train that was late. He jumped from the train into a taxi and said to the chauffeur, "Drive fast, step on it!" And the taxi driver did. He stepped on it. And when after some fifteen minutes, speeding through the streets and skidding around corners, the lecturer said, "Well, aren't we about there?" the taxi driver said, "I don't know, sir. You never told me where we were to go." Some people are like that, busy, hectic, with no determining aim to guide their hurried lives. Many, however—and one suspects that more of them are here today—are of another sort altogether. They do have fine ideals, grand intentions in general for their lives and families, but alas! they have never faced up to the basic meaning of a law-abiding universe where no idealistic desire alone ever yet carried anyone to any good destination on the wrong bus. Such folk need to confront, not so much the question of fine aims and high ideals, as the question concerning the road they are practically traveling today. Ask any scientist in his laboratory about this. He wants something; above all else he wants to discover something and get somewhere; there are thousands of ways of missing it, just one way of finding it, one set of conditions to be fulfilled if he is ever to achieve it. Do we suppose that that fact applies in the physical realm and not in the spiritual? In this regard Jesus was a scientist before science came, laying down the laws of the spiritual realm and insisting that the conditions must be fulfilled. "Narrow is the gate, and straitened the way, that leadeth unto life."

Consider further that we face here not only the profound implication of a law-abiding universe but one of the most searching tests of our own personal sincerity. It is one thing, and comparatively easy too, to desire something ideal and right; it is another thing to be willing to pay the price. At that point hypocrisy flourishes. Many people who weigh two hundred and fifty pounds desire in general to weigh one hundred and fifty, but the price! One look at them reveals that they do not really desire to weigh one hundred and fifty pounds. Narrow is the gate, and straitened the way.

When from such homely matters one carries this truth up into life's most exalted realms the same fact holds. Professor Mortimer Adler of the University of Chicago says that ultimately mankind will achieve a world permanently at peace, but that it will take five hundred years to do it. That is just the time Thomas Jefferson said it would take American civilization to reach the Pacific coast. In his *Notes On Virginia* Jefferson said it would take two hundred years before we reached the Mississippi and between two and three hundred years more before the conquest of the continent reached the Pacific. It was less than a hundred and fifty years ago he said that, and we have been on the Pacific a long time now. Perhaps we can beat the timetable again in building a world order that will assure peace, but it is going to cost a kind of wise and sacrificial devotion the nations now are not exhibiting. "My friend," Du Pont de Nemours once wrote to Thomas Jefferson, "we are but snails, and we have to climb the Cordillera!" And then he added five words like the crack of a whip: "By God! We must climb!"

In every realm the truth holds: "Wide is the gate, and broad is the way, that leadeth to destruction, and many are they that enter in thereby. For narrow is the gate, and straitened the way, that leadeth unto life, and few are they that find it." All great achievement—intellectual, artistic, spiritual, ethical—is reached in Jesus' meaning of the word, not by a broad, loose meandering road, but by a narrow way.

Concentration is narrow. Gladstone, asked the secret of his successful career, answered with one word: "Concentration!" *Decision* is narrow. When one decides, one gives up vagueness and generalities, and becomes particular and concrete. *Self-discipline* is narrow. Ask a man like Toscanini what it means! No broad road for a loose, meandering gypsy to travel on ever led to such artistry as his. *Loyalty* is narrow. It binds us to definite devotions. The man who swears allegiance to a cause has limitations stronger than a slave's because his heart is given. When I love my friend I am not loosely free; I do not want to be loosely free; my limitation is my glory, I love my friend. But the unloyal man travels a broad road; he has no attachments; he is devoted to no friend; he is a man without a country. "Wide is the gate, and broad is the way."

Here, then, is a central test of our personal sincerity—we who so easily profess Christian ideals for ourselves, our families and our world—are we willing to pay the price?

This test is going to come sternly home to us as a nation, desiring as we do a world organized for peace. Granted, that that desire in general is widespread, deep-seated, strong. It had better be, for many reasons, and for one reason in particular that I have never heard anybody mention. In ancient Greek times the average age of death in the population was about twenty-nine. In Massachusetts, in 1800, the average age of death was about thirty-five. As late as 1890 in the United States the average age of death was forty-three. So in that old world of our fathers, the men who planned wars fought them. The same age group that said, We must go to war, shouldered the guns and went. But now with the average age of death away up in the sixties, we—millions upon millions of older folk—may say war, but then not we but our sons and daughters go out to fight it. We, the elders, pick out our finest, bravest, most promising youths and send them out to fight while we stay home. It is an intolerable situation, the older age group more and more controlling the policies of nations, and the younger age group bearing the terrific burden of the consequence. Who of us elders would not gladly lay down his life to save from death some promising youth, his valuable life still ahead of him, whom we have sent out to fight? But we cannot do it. Modern war presents the older generation with a heartbreaking situation. Of course we desire a world organized for peace! Never was that desire stronger or more universal. But the test of our sincerity in desiring it still lies ahead of us. Are we as a nation going to be willing to pay the price?

As for personal life, God grant that each one here may apply this to himself! Fine ideals, good desires in general—we are taking that for granted. But at that point the question of sincerity rises. Which bus are we on, now, this morning, in our practical, immediate habits and ways of living? Are some of us on the wrong bus?

Obviously we are dealing here with one of the commonest causes of brokenhearted regret and penitence. It is so easy to catch the wrong bus. We do it when we do not mean to. We get on it without realizing we are there, not at all surrendering our fine dreams and aims but all the time thinking, like that man going to Detroit, that we are headed where we want to go, whereas we are really going somewhere else. How many such cases a personal counselor sees!

A family comes to New York, a fine family with high ideals for themselves and their children. Make a direct attack on their ideals and one would be met with stout resistance. They do desire a happy, united, loyal, respected, Christian home, fully intending to ally themselves with the best in the community, the church and social service, fine friends and great opportunities. But in New York there are a lot of buses running. I almost hesitate to describe one of them lest some should think that I am turning Puritan. I am not. I am just describing what I see—that night club, cocktail hour, drink-because-others-do, and don't-be-prudish-because-it-makes-you-seem-queer way of living. So this family, not consciously surrendering a single one of its high ideals, boards that bus—not so bad at first, but not so good either—and travels without recognizing it far away from the decent moral standards that are the underpinning of any strong and lovely home. And then some day that bus reaches its destination. Alas! that was not where they had intended to land. "There is a way," says the Scripture, "which seemeth right unto a man, but the end thereof are the ways of death."

This kind of experience in family and personal life more than any other makes a man call himself a fool. A sinner? Yes. But sometimes I think a man can face having been a sinner and still retain some self-respect. To have had fine aims, however, good intentions, high ideals, and then like an idiot to have caught the wrong bus—the most ashamed people I ever see are those who thus blame themselves for being fools.

Do you young people still read De Maupassant's stories? Brilliant, clever, gay, often ribald and indecent, no one can read them without seeing behind them a young man, his heart set on a free, full, happy life. But no one can read them either without guessing what bus he himself had boarded and wondering where it landed him in the end. I never knew what happened to De Maupassant until the other day. It was all over for him by the time he was forty-three. His biographer says: "By 1891 he was a wreck . . . The story of his last years makes painful reading. In 1892 he was committed to a private asylum. On July 6 of the following year the end came." So, he headed for a full, free, happy life, but he caught the wrong bus.

Thus we come to the consequence of the matter. One of the most crucial needs of the world today, personal, domestic, national, international, is the re-establishment of Christian moral standards. They have been dreadfully shaken. The whole Nazi movement was built upon the proposition that there were no such standards, things everlastingly right and everlastingly wrong, with God himself pledged to see to it that nothing traveling a wrong road ever comes to a right end. Beneath the urgent political needs of the time for international organization and all the rest is this fundamental need, the re-establishment of moral standards, and moral standards have their inception, their development and their confirmation, inside the lives of individuals. Take it for granted that we desire good goals—happiness, prosperity, peace. But our immediate volition cannot deal directly with goals; our immediate volition has to deal, here and now, with the choice of means, with the road we start on, with the bus we board. In God's name, let us look to it, lest having desired great things we discover again that hell can be paved with good intentions! For the gospel is that there is a right way, offered us in Christ. It does cost concentration, decision, self-discipline, loyalty, as everything most worth while in man's experience does, but it leads to life. I want some choices made here this morning, that years from now, when the trip is done, will land us where we really want to go, knowing for ourselves the meaning of the Master's word, "I am the way."

The Great Hours of a Man's Life

IN THE twelfth chapter of Second Corinthians, Paul describes one of the great hours in his experience: "I know a man in Christ, fourteen years ago (whether in the body, I know not; or whether out of the body, I know not; God knoweth), such a one caught up even to the third heaven. And I know such a man (whether in the body, or apart from the body, I know not; God knoweth), how that he was caught up into Paradise, and heard unspeakable words, which it is not lawful for a man to utter." That must have been a high hour of insight and vision, and described though it is in ancient symbolism, we all know at least a little what it means. Our spiritual lives, too, have times when vision clears, and doubt and cynicism go, and our souls are kindled and aflame. We may prefer Browning's way of describing them—

> "moments,
> Sure tho' seldom, ...
> When the spirit's true endowments
> Stand out plainly from its false ones"—

but however we may describe them, we know what such experiences mean.

Now at the time when Paul recalled that great hour of his he was in one of the most despondent periods of his life—not having a great hour at all. In the verses immediately preceding, he recounts his tribulations—labor and travail, hunger and thirst, cold and nakedness, and, "Besides those things that are without," he adds, "that which presseth upon me daily, anxiety for all the churches." Paul is in a down hour. In words that suggest our situation now, he describes his time. "Quarrels," he says, "jealousy, temper, rivalry, slanders, gossiping, arro-

gance, and disorder." Such, in this very chapter, is Paul's list
of the evils of his time.

Then into the midst of his discouraging present he interjects
a factor that makes all the difference in the world to him. His
high hours and what they have taught him, come back to him.
Fourteen years before, he recalls one of them when vision cleared
and the eternal verities were surely seen. Like a sailor on a
foggy day having a tough time, he remembers his clear days
when far horizons could be seen. And as one reads this worried
letter, written out of a disheartening present, one sees this thing
at least that is saving the man and making him rememberable
yet across the centuries: he is believing the testimony of his
best hours against the testimony of his worst hours as to what
life really means.

Is not that one of the central problems of human life? Which
are we to believe, our best hours or our worst? We have them
both. We may be a long way from mystics, not given to spiritual
raptures but, matter of fact and pedestrian though our tempera-
ments may be, we do have hours when life seems meaningful,
goodness beautiful, love the greatest thing in the world, God
real, and the victory of righteousness a possibility worth living
and dying for. But then low hours also come. Man's stupidity
and brutality are dreadful; they dishearten us. Good plans for
peace and decency go awry; wars are won, but disillusionment
follows victory, and cynicism seems at times the only realism.
This alternation of mood characterizes every life. As the Negro
spiritual says,

> "Sometimes I'se up, sometimes I'se down,
>   Oh, yes, Lord."

A decisive question rises, therefore, on whose answer depends
the total meaning of one's life—which do we really believe and
trust and base our lives upon, the testimony of the high hours, or
of the low?

Surely, we need Paul's secret now. Many of us here are

in a low mood, in a depressing year. We have won a war, but what a mess! It is foggy weather on a rough sea for all of us who care about the world, and I, for one, need to remember the clear days when I could see better. This morning let us consider what that might mean to us.

First of all, recall those better hours so that they may be real to us. I do not mean simply happy hours, when all was going well, but better hours, when great things seemed great and life was purposeful, when worth-while endeavors challenged us, and we were our best selves.

One of my boyhood's recollections is my father dealing with me when I was in a bad temper. "Where's Harry?" he would say, and I would answer, "Why, here he is." And he would say to me, "No! You are not Harry. Harry is lost. Go find him. I want Harry!" So, catching his meaning, I would wander off through the house, getting myself under control until, returning, I could face him again, saying, "I've found him. Here he is." Thus my father said to me, as a child, what modern psychology is saying now—that we are not just one self, but varied selves, high and low, good and bad, and that the art of life is to identify oneself with one's best self, and believe and be what that best self affirms. What my father said to me sixty years ago I am trying now to say to myself, in a depressing year when one's best self is sometimes hard to find.

Biography is a running commentary on this matter. Wordsworth, for example, had great hours:

> "I have felt
> A presence that disturbs me with the joy
> Of elevated thoughts";—

hours like that!

> "While with an eye made quiet by the power
> Of harmony, and the deep power of joy,
> We see into the life of things"—

hours like that!

"There are times,
I doubt not, when to you it doth impart
Authentic tidings of invisible things"—
hours like that!

Wordsworth, however, did not always have such hours. The French Revolution aroused his ardent hopes. To it his faith was given; a brave new era, so he thought, was coming. Then post-war letdown came, disillusioning, frightening, and Wordsworth cried:

"I lost
All feeling of conviction, and, in fine,
Sick, wearied out with contrarieties,
Yielded up moral questions in despair."

That's Wordsworth, too! Well, in Wordsworth, as in all of us, there is plenty to criticize—he did not make a perfect score—yet, thinking now of his life's total meaning, here is his glory, that on the whole he stands in mankind's recollection for his best hours, that in the long run what his great days said he believed and caused to be remembered. That is the mark of high character.

Here is a strange mystery in human nature, that with an inner certainty none can deny, we do distinguish our best hours from our worst. Sir Edward Elgar wrote a lot of music, more or less good, but once, in "The Dream of Gerontius," he composed something that he knew was his very best. "This is the best of me," he wrote to a friend, "for the rest, I ate, and drank, and slept, and loved and hated, like another; my life was as the vapour, and is not; *but this I saw and knew;* this, if anything of mine, is worth your memory." Every one of us knows what Elgar meant, and his was Paul's experience over again. Paul knew his best when it came. What he saw on the Damascus Road; what he felt when he wrote the thirteenth chapter of First Corinthians; what he knew when he answered the call of the man of Macedonia, "Come over and help us"; what he beheld when he was, as it were, caught up into the third heaven—that was his best and, come what low moods might, he would believe that, take that for the interpretation of his life. How we need now to make our own that secret of great character!

See now that when we talk thus about what our best hours reveal, we are really talking about essential Christianity. The Christian view of God and man and life's meaning, is the outlook of our best hours. It is when we are crushed and cynical that we say, I cannot believe in a good God and in the Christian way of life. Sometimes we consider that an argument against Christianity. But, friends, that is an argument for Christianity. It is when we are down and out, beaten in spirit and at our worst, that we say we cannot believe in God and his Christ. But when great hours come, and the fog departs and vision clears, then the higher the mood reaches the more possible and real Christian faith appears. This is the stubborn fact on which all attacks on Christianity ultimately go to pieces, that in our best hours the Christian view of life is most real.

So Ernest Renan said, "Man is most religious in his best moments." So Browning sang:

"Faith is my waking life:
One sleeps, indeed, and dreams at intervals,
We know, but waking's the main point with us."

So even Tyndall, the nineteenth century scientist, regarded by Christians of his day as a materialist and their mortal enemy, said once about the materialistic philosophy, "I have noticed during years of self-observation, that it is not in hours of clearness and vigor that this doctrine commends itself to my mind."

I should say not! We have low hours when nothing seems real except the physical, but then great hours come and lo! the soul is real again. We have low hours when we feel like crying, There is no God! but then high hours come, when we know that life must be purposeful, divine meaning in it, Providence over it,

God in control of it. We have low hours when man seems only an educated brute, but then great hours come when love of man grows real again and we see him as a child of God, appallingly wayward, but with his sonship still the deepest fact about him. I am appealing now to no ecclesiastical or creedal authority but to the authority of our own enlightened hours. It is they which bear witness to the truth of Christ.

One of the strangest statements from an early church father is Tertullian's saying that the human soul is "naturally Christian." What can he mean by that? Does not Christianity teach that man is naturally corrupt? Are not the doctrines of original sin and of total depravity, orthodox Christian teaching? How can Tertullian, seeing human nature as he saw it in the brutal days of the Roman Empire, say that the human soul is naturally Christian? But he said it, and what he meant we are trying to say today. Catch man in his best hours and see how Christian his thoughts, his ideals, his aspirations, his convictions are!

We ask too much if we expect not to have low hours. In every realm they come. Would you not say that of all men who ever lived Wordsworth most surely would always respond to nature's beauties? But he didn't!

> "There was a time when meadow, grove, and stream,
> The earth, and every common sight,
>   To me did seem
>   Appareled in celestial light,
> The glory and the freshness of a dream.
> It is not now as it hath been of yore;—
>   Turn whereso'er I may,
>   By night or day,
> The things which I have seen I now can see no more."

Even in his love of nature Wordsworth had low hours. The question is not whether such times come, but whether, when they come, we are at their mercy. We need not be at their mercy.

When they come we can still trust and base our lives upon our hours of insight.

Ah, Paul, you were up against this! "Fourteen years ago," you wrote, remembering back so far to a day of clear vision you could trust. You were a Christian through thick and thin, "in season and out of season," as the letter to Timothy says, because you trusted your enlightened not your darkened hours.

Very pertinent to us now is the third truth with which our theme confronts us, namely, that it is crisis that often calls the great hours out. Throughout this sermon we have spoken of these present days as depressing, but that is not the whole truth. Again and again in history, it is the critical periods that have called out the great hours.

In personal life this is true. Some of us never rise to our great hours until we are up against something difficult. Sidney Lanier, stricken with tuberculosis, was banished from his work to win his hard battle if he could, and there in the crisis of his life he had an unforgettable experience, which he made immortal in his lines about the hour when

> ". . . belief overmasters doubt, and I know that I know,
> And my spirit is grown to a lordly great compass
> within."

Crisis can call out great hours.

In every realm this is about the most encouraging aspect of history. We are still playing Hamlet in New York City. We go back yet to that amazing outburst of creative literature in the Elizabethan era. But what an unsettled age it was! Columbus discovered America, and a whole new world was opened up. Twenty-five years after that, Luther nailed his theses to the Cathedral doors at Wittenberg, and the Reformation began its tumultuous career. Wars raged, new adventures were called for, new adjustments demanded. It was an uproarious century.

And then, out of that tremendous era came what Tennyson called

> "Those melodious bursts that fill
> The spacious times of great Elizabeth
> With sounds that echo still."

What is true in literature is true in every creative realm of the spirit. Crisis can call out great hours.

Let us say this to ourselves now! This is a time for greatness. God grant us statesmen to measure up to it! But if our children, looking back on our days, are going to think of them as a great era in history—crisis turned into opportunity—there must be at the heart of this generation enough individuals who make that response in their own living.

Our Lord himself faced this. He had low hours too. If ever a soul might have been expected to live always on the heights it was he. But not even he could do it. "Now is my soul troubled; and what shall I say? Father, save me from this hour." He too had days of fog on a dangerous sea. He had memorized—mark it —he had memorized the Psalm which begins,

> "My God, my God, why hast thou forsaken me?
> Why art thou so far from helping me, and from
>   the words of my groaning?"

Our Lord was transfigured, we say, until the fashion of his countenance was altered—yes—but only once—once!

> "Tasks in hours of insight will'd
> Can be through hours of gloom fulfill'd."

Matthew Arnold said that, but Jesus knew its meaning. To follow in his steps means this too—to believe in our enlightened hours when days are dark and to use crisis, even though it be a cross, to make the great hours come.

So may God grant this inward victory to each of us!

A Man Is What He Proves To Be in an Emergency

JUDGING by letters from the radio audience, no verse in the Bible puzzles more people than the petition in the Lord's Prayer, "Lead us not into temptation." Is it not a shocking idea, many say, that God leads men into temptation, and that we must beg him to stop doing it? Since we repeat it so often, it is worth while clearing up the meaning of this phrase, especially since few passages in the New Testament are so directly applicable as this one is to our situation now.

Our English rendering, "Lead us not into temptation," is, of course, a translation from the Greek, and the Greek in turn a translation from the Aramaic that Jesus spoke. Our English word "temptation" has come to mean almost exclusively seduction to moral wickedness, and our trouble with this text begins to clear up when we go back to the Greek word, whose primary meaning is not that at all. The Greek word basically means "trial" of any sort, moral or otherwise—adversity, difficulty, critical emergency that tests a man so that under its strain he is likely to go to pieces. Sometimes in the New Testament our standard English translations render this Greek word by our word "temptation," and sometimes by our word "trial," and it is a pity they did not use that latter word in the Lord's Prayer. When Paul, for example, writes of the "trials which befell me"; when Peter writes of being "put to grief in manifold trials"; when in the Book of Revelation God promises, "I . . . will keep thee from the hour of trial"; and when Jesus said to his disciples, "Ye are they that have continued with me in my temptations" —that is, my difficulties, struggles, times of testing—this same Greek word is being rendered. Did not the Master when he faced the cross, pray, "If it be possible, let this cup pass from me"? So he tells his disciples to pray that deeply human prayer, which must spring from the heart of every man today: Spare us these terrific testings that shake men's souls to pieces, but, if that is not possible, then deliver us from evil.

Moreover, our English phrase, "Lead us not," as though God were dragging us into trial, is too strong. The Revised version says, "Bring us not," and a better rendering yet is now suggested: "Let us not enter into trial."

Of course the Lord's Prayer does not mean that God seduces men to sin! "Let no man say when he is tempted," writes James, "I am tempted of God; for God cannot be tempted with evil, and he himself tempteth no man." Concerning this all scholars agree; what they differ about is the Aramaic words that Jesus himself used, of which the Greek is a translation. Dr. Torrey of Yale, for example, feels sure that Jesus used another Aramaic word altogether than has been commonly supposed, so that he translates this prayer, "Let us not yield to temptation, but deliver us from evil."

In any case the major consequence is clear. This petition in the Lord's Prayer is a cry out of the deeps of man's soul, very relevant to our situation now. Whether it means, "Let us not yield to temptation," or, "Spare us from times of testing, but deliver us from evil," who of us does not need to have that prayer answered?

What we really are always comes out in the testing of emergency. Any sailor is safe in a mild breeze; how much of a sailor he is, is revealed when a storm puts him to the test. Well, the storm has landed on us. Heaven knows we prayed to escape it, but we are in the thick of it now, with the need deep in all of us: Let us fail not in the time of testing.

This morning, then, we consider some basic conditions within ourselves that must be fulfilled if that prayer is to be answered.

For one thing, never think of a time of testing as tragedy alone. This catastrophe we face can easily take on in our imagination the aspect and proportion of an earthquake, a monstrous tragedy too huge to be our fault or our responsibility, something we did not cause and can do little to affect. So fatalistically pictured, our disaster calls out an unhappy series of negative responses. Some collapse and feel they cannot stand it; some grow cynical and lose all faith in so diabolical a world; some fall back on self-pity and feel dreadfully sorry for themselves; some grow hard and stoical and grit their teeth. How natural such negative responses are! How real the temptation to be content with them!

Turn to the Bible, however, which, from beginning to end faces catastrophe, and one finds another kind of simile in which the great souls behind the book pictured the meaning of disaster. To be sure, the earthquake figure is there: "Therefore will not we fear, though the earth be removed, and though the mountains be carried into the midst of the sea . . . The Lord of hosts is with us; the God of Jacob is our refuge." Men such as that Psalmist did rise to heights where even when they faced catastrophe like an earthquake they met the test with faith and courage. But why they met it so is explained in part by other similes, in which they symbolized what they thought disaster really means.

"A refiner's fire"—that is a common figure of speech. When trouble comes, they said, it can separate the gold in us from the alloy, bringing out the best and destroying the worst. "Tribulation"—that is another common simile; it means "threshing." When disaster falls it is like the flail on a threshing floor; it can separate the grain in us from the chaff, bring out our finest, throw away our worst. "Chastening"—that is another common simile: "Whom the Lord loveth he chasteneth." So, they said, God cannot let us get away scatheless with our iniquity, and when disaster comes, the consequence of our human folly and wickedness, as this catastrophe of ours is now, it is more than tragedy; it is chastening, from which, if we are wise, we can learn the lessons we most deeply need to learn. As Sir Humphry Davy once said about his scientific discoveries: "The most important of my discoveries have been suggested to me by failures."

It does make a difference in what terms we picture our times of testing. A refiner's fire that can bring out the gold, a threshing floor that can reveal the wheat, chastening that can teach us life's great lessons—if our disaster means that to us, then in us the Lord's Prayer can be answered.

In 1891 there was in Cambridge University a student named Edward Wilson, whom his associates nicknamed, "Bill the Cynic." He was not a very agreeable young fellow and he had a bitter tongue. He wrote once to a friend whom he had offended, "I know I am hard, proud, conceited, scornful, bitter and hard and insulting very often, and always selfish; but I don't like you to treat me as though I wasn't trying to do a bit better." That same Edward Wilson was later the physician of Captain Scott's expedition to the South Pole. They called him, "Bill the Peacemaker," and this is what Captain Scott wrote about him in that last hour when they lay dying amid the antarctic snow: "If this letter reaches you, Bill and I will have gone out together. We are very near it now; and I should like you to know how splendid he was at the end, everlastingly cheerful and ready to sacrifice himself for others. His eyes have a comfortable blue look of hope, and his mind is peaceful with the satisfaction of his faith in regarding himself as part of the great scheme of the Almighty."

So, gold does come from a refiner's fire, wheat from a threshing floor, wisdom from chastening; and thus to see the positive possibilities in our times of trial opens at least the chance of the Lord's Prayer being answered in us: "Grant that we fail not in the time of testing, but deliver us from evil."

As a help in achieving this victory, a second factor is important: bulwarking ourselves with great examples of those in whom this prayer was answered. In the New Testament, the letter to the Hebrews was written just as persecution of the Christians was getting under way. They had not yet "resisted unto blood," the writer said, but the prospect of it was close

[154]

around the corner, and the writer was anxious that the church should not fail in the test. To that end he argued earnestly, presenting the profound truths and resources of the gospel, but he did something else too which shows him to be a good psychologist as well as a good Christian. In his magnificent eleventh chapter he marshalled the heroes of the faith and set them marching through the imagination of those early Christians, men and women of whom the world was not worthy, who turned disaster into gain, enduring insufferable trials, "as seeing him who is invisible." What a stirring company they are! They doubtless prayed the human prayer, "Let us not enter into trial," yet when trial came, resolute and strong, they prayed the rest of the petition, "but deliver us from evil." Still across centuries that picture the writer to the Hebrews drew is vivid: the amphitheater, with the athletic contests on and the great host of spectators filling all the seats, while the exhortation sounds, "Seeing we are compassed about with so great a cloud of witnesses, . . . let us run with patience the race that is set before us."

I, for one, need today the stimulus of such great examples. This wartime strain and its post-war aftermath have been borne especially by the young—alas, most terribly by the young! But we elders too are tempted. It is not easy to see the hopes of a lifetime foiled, the ideals to which long years have been given violated, and to face a world whose chaos we will not outlive. It would be all too easy for our spirits to fail, and when such hours come it is generally not arguments that help so much, as examples.

Once there was a young man in Springfield, Illinois, who ran for the legislature and was defeated. Then he entered business, and failed, and spent seventeen years paying the debts of a worthless partner. He fell passionately in love with the girl of his choice who loved him in return, and then she died. He was elected to Congress in 1846 and served one term but was defeated when he ran for re-election. Next, he tried to get an appointment to the United States Land Office and failed. Then, becoming a candidate for the United States Senate, he was defeated. In 1856 as a candidate for the vice presidency he was beaten, and two years later Douglas defeated him again. And when at last he became President, the first thing that happened was a great war that he would have given his life to prevent. What a lifetime of testing! But in Washington there is a Memorial to him that some of us can hardly enter without tears, and in the heart of the nation and of the world a more enduring memorial that will last forever. How often he prayed, "Spare me the time of testing," and yet how splendidly he finished it: "but deliver me from evil."

Seeing disaster as a refiner's fire that can bring out our gold, bulwarked by great examples in whose spiritual companionship we live, consider now another factor that contributes to the answering of this prayer: loyalty to others that displaces pity for ourselves. We rightly emphasize the divine resources that sustained the Master when he faced the cross, but along with them was his loyalty to those disciples whom he loved. "For their sakes," he cried, "I sanctify (that is, dedicate) myself." So he escaped the weakness of self-pity because he was absorbed in loyalty to others; for their sakes he met the time of testing.

Stories from the battlefront have revealed how powerfully this motive operated there. Terrific emergencies that men could never meet for their own sakes alone, they met superbly because they were thinking of their fellows whom they would not let down. We commonly present unselfishness as a lovely virtue. So it is, but it is more than that. Watch some man meet an emergency where you might expect him to go to pieces, and if instead he pulls himself together, surmounting it with superb courage, you may be sure of one thing—that man was thinking of someone else whom he would not let down. Unselfishness is not simply lovely. In many a man today, rising to meet ghastly times of testing, the source of strength is in an attitude that we too often think of as merely a beautiful ideal: "For their sakes I dedicate myself."

To us also who are older this truth applies. I must confess, for one, that were I to think of myself alone I should often find it hard to keep going. What's the use? Even the Psalmist had a weak moment when he said: "The days of our years are three-score years and ten; and if by reason of strength they be four-score years, yet is their strength labour and sorrow; for it is soon cut off, and we fly away." But suppose a man stops think-ing only of himself! There are the children, for example. Above all else, there are the children! What kind of world will they have to grow up in? One must not let the children down. One must do all one can to help build a world where they will not have to face what we are facing. Let one think of the children and one's chin does go up, and purpose, resolution, capacity for work and sacrifice come back again. This crisis is not simply tragedy; it is opportunity.

> "There is a tide in the affairs of men
> Which taken at the flood leads on to fortune;
> Omitted, all the voyage of their life
> Is bound in shallows and in miseries."

Such is the crisis of our time, with the good fortune or disaster of our children depending on the way we handle it. Let enough people so see our era, and the Lord's Prayer will be answered: "Let us not yield to temptation."

All this, however, leads to the final matter. If that prayer is to be answered, dig deep into the divine resources, the eternal purpose backed by the Eternal Power that can sustain us in the toughest trials and that all these temporal adversities in the end cannot defeat. In Narvik, Norway, when things were at their worst, the Nazis in control, their calculated cruelty doing abominable things, and in addition the Allies bombing the city to pieces to get them out, the mayor of Narvik said to a group of newspaper men, "The mountains are still ours." So, the Eternal regnant above the temporal has sustained souls in whom the Lord's Prayer has been answered. The mountains were still theirs.

One feels sorry for some people today. They have never known what vital Christianity means, and now they face an emergency. And when an emergency comes there is so little time to get ready. One must be ready. Life is a series of ambushes. Trouble commonly does not evolve by slow gradations; it rather leaps upon us, and when that happens there is so little time to get ready—one must be ready. This is true in ordinary days, but it is accentuated now. When that letter from the War Office came to our homes—"We regret to inform you"—it came, not gradually, but suddenly. So all life in general and these days in particular teach the need of deep, abiding spiritual foundations under life, so that when suddenly the rains descend, the floods come, and the winds blow and beat upon our house, we may stand the test.

When the Nazis took over Holland one of the first cases of resistance they met was in an official at the Hague. The Nazis commanded him to inquire of any person applying for a position whether the applicant had Jewish ancestry, and this official called his staff together and said, "As a confessing Christian and as a Dutchman I cannot ask anyone this question. It is against the deepest foundations of our faith in Jesus Christ, in whom God reveals himself to all men and before whom all men are equal, to prefer one man to another because he belongs to a certain race or a certain nationality." So he stood his ground and they sent him to a concentration camp. When the sudden testing came, he was ready.

So, too, Jesus went into the Garden of Gethsemane. There was no time to learn to pray. Thank God, he had prayed all his life! Before the crisis fell he was already in touch with the eternal resources. He was ready. And the prayer he had taught to his disciples, he prayed then: If it be possible, spare me this time of testing—but! but deliver me from evil.

Resources for Life's Mastery

MARK TWAIN once wrote in his notebook that every year millions of people die who, as they come to the end, scoff at life in their hearts. "Scoff," he says, "at the pitiful world, and the useless universe and violent, contemptible human race," deriding "the whole paltry scheme." Indeed, despite his sense of humor, his flair for fun, that is pretty much the way Mark Twain himself felt at the end. Preachers commonly divide men into good and bad, but then one runs upon two different kinds of good men, those who end with the cynicism Mark Twain describes and those who crown life's close with radiance and zest. On one side Clarence Darrow, a good man, with an eminent career, says as he reaches life's conclusion, "The outstanding fact that cannot be dodged by thoughtful men is the futility of it all," while another good man, Robert Louis Stevenson, long familiar with hardship, says, "Sick and well, I have had a splendid life of it, grudge nothing, regret very little." What a difference between two kinds of good men!

Considering this contrast, it is evident that every life has two aspects, the objective and the subjective—first, the impact on us of external circumstance, and then our own subjective contribution, our inner dealing with it all, our spiritual attitude toward life and interpretation of it. And watching these two factors operate the impression grows that with most of us it is mainly our inward, subjective contribution that in the end determines what life means to us.

"I have overcome the world," said Jesus. Well, he did gloriously overcome it! Yet, judging by his life's objective facts, he had ample reason to scoff at the pitiful world and the violent, contemptible human race. His victory was inward, not so much circumstance as his own attitude toward life and interpretation of it producing the amazing consequence.

[159]

Since this is to be our emphasis, we must guard ourselves against seeming to minimize the importance of external circumstance. It must not be minimized. It can be utterly crushing, until life has no chance at all. Anne O'Hare McCormick, of the New York Times, returning from Europe, says, "One of the worst tragedies in Europe is the 5-year-old-people who look like 70, because they have seen things no child ever should see." God forbid that in times like these we should minimize what outward circumstance can do to life, blasting its hopes beyond remedy until no subjective contribution one can reasonably expect can redeem the soul from ruin and despair! Few if any of us, however, are in such a case. Still, in us, not one factor only, the objective, determines our life's quality and meaning, but two factors: first, the objective, but then what inwardly we do with it, what attitudes we take toward it, what interpretations we give to it. It is there, within ourselves, that we win or lose our battle for life's mastery.

Considering these subjective factors, it is clear, for one thing, that a man's will power is involved. In estimating Jesus' character we habitually stress the other aspects of his personality—his mind, revealing truth the centuries confirm, and his emotions, deep, compassionate, humane. Too often we neglect his decisive, indefatigable power of will, setting out to do something with his life that hell and high water could not stop. In no small measure this quality in him made those first disciples feel toward him as Kent felt toward King Lear:

> ". . . you have that in your countenance
> which I would fain call master."

In us, too, strong volition is called for in so dealing with life as to make it meaningful and radiant. Two men, for example, are told by their physicians that they have only a few more months to live. The same fact faces both. Whereupon the first man collapses into plaintiveness and fear, while the second, like one I knew who now has fallen on sleep, so deals with that same fact that his family, far from having to support his spirit, are supported by it. He even capitalizes the forbidding event, making those final months among the most rememberable and influential of his life, and he goes out on his adventure as though the old hymn told the truth:

> "It were a well spent journey
> Though seven deaths lay between."

Those two men illustrate our thesis, that not objective fact so much as our subjective attitude determines the total quality of our experience, and everyone must feel in that second man the drive of a strong will.

Nevertheless, if this were all one had to say it would be thin gospel. George Eliot as a young woman wanted above all else to marry Herbert Spencer. Moreover, for years he played around with her until all their friends supposed that of course they would marry. One day, however, he took a shilling and flipped it; heads he would marry, tails he would not; and it came down tails. Months afterwards, out of her convalescence from heartbreak the young woman who was later to be George Eliot wrote to a friend, "I am very well and 'plucky'—a word which I propose to substitute for happy, as more truthful." Well, in these days everyone needs pluck, and that is a matter of will power; but thank God, there is more to say than that!

Study the difference between these two types of people we are considering, and deeper than will power one keeps finding a divergence in their philosophies of life. Clarence Darrow was a skeptic, an agnostic; Robert Louis Stevenson believed, as he said, in "an ultimate decency of things." "Aye," he wrote, "and if I woke in hell, should still believe it!" What we are driving at this morning is especially pertinent to our time. The objective facts of this generation are terrific; yet all of us want to come to the end of our days with lives meaningful and radiant. In achieving that we cannot count on the objective factors alone to produce it. Not in these days! We must count upon our own subjective attitude, and at the heart of that is our philosophy of life, what we do honestly think life ultimately means.

Philosophy is commonly supposed to be a recondite affair for experts only, but it isn't. Every man of us day by day is working out his philosophy, his interpretation of the facts of life. The idea in many people's minds in this scientific age has been that science gives us all the facts, that facts are all we need, that when we have the facts we have all that we can know. But when we have all the facts, what about the interpretation of the facts? Life's whole meaning hinges on that.

Here, for example, are the discoverable facts about the origins of this universe. But listen to the contrasting interpretations: one materialist saying, "It is all an affair of chance, the froth and fume of the waves on an ocean of sterile matter," while others, great scientists—Compton, Jeans and the rest—say that it cannot be chance; they believe in God. Both sets of men face the same facts, but with what different interpretations!

Or take a detail in life, like the sense of duty. What do you make of it, this strange, commanding, imperative sense of moral obligation in us? Haeckel, the materialist, calls it merely a physical accident, due, he says, to "a long series of phyletic modifications of the phronema of the cortex," while Wordsworth says,

"Stern Daughter of the Voice of God!
O Duty!"

Haeckel and Wordsworth faced the same fact, but what a difference in interpretation!

Or consider mankind's strange history upon this planet and see what diverse meanings can be given it. "Our entire human adventure here is a side show on a ridiculous star," says one, while Paul discerned in it what he called the eternal purpose which God purposed in Christ. That difference lies not in the ascertainable facts but in their interpretation.

Or think of someone's death, someone close to us and in-finitely dear. There the fact stares us in the face. But as to its meaning, James Thomson says life

> ". . . grinds him some slow years of bitter breath,
> Then grinds him back into eternal death,"

while the New Testament says, "This mortal must put on im-mortality."

Whatever else is clear from this power of interpretation we inwardly exercise one thing is obvious: humans are not like the animals. An event befalls an animal and when the animal is through with it, it is the same event it was before. But the same kind of event befalls a man and at once something begins to hap-pen to it; the man's interpretations get to work on it; it comes out of that man's life something quite other than it was when it went in, changed by his responses, attitudes, explanations. In man's life, every experience has two aspects, the outer fact and the inner interpretation.

At this point each of us confronts the question, not what is life doing to us but what are we doing to life by the way we look at it? We can make life meaningless or glorious by our interpretations. The objective facts of experience come to each of us, like a font of type, and if we live long enough we are likely to get all the letters of the alphabet, and then by our handling of them we set that type up one way or another. Macbeth, calling life

> " . . . a tale
> Told by an idiot, full of sound and fury,
> Signifying nothing,"

is using exactly the same letters that Jesus' noblest words are set in. So the same objective facts we subjectively interpret to mean either blasting cynicism or ennobling faith. Every day, one way or another, we all are doing that.

In these days I thank God for the Christian philosophy of

life and for the privilege of having preached it these forty years and more. We desperately need it if we are to see this generation through! Will power is not enough; it was not enough for Christ; he saw life at its damnedest, faced it at its cruelest, and rose above it, transformed it, glorified it. His deep convictions about God and God's purpose and life's eternal meaning, saw him through. A few weeks ago my friend fell on sleep. I knew him well. He was a real Christian. I saw him once go through a difficult experience of a kind that bowls even strong men over, and he was handling it with such poise, such gallantry and good will that I praised him for it. "Harry," he said in answer, "I have a philosophy of life that sees me through." So may God grant to us in days like these!

Nevertheless, even this is not enough. Watch these men and women who come through hard experiences in difficult generations with heads unbowed and hearts uncrushed, and one habitually discerns in them an experience of contact—vital, inward contact—with a power greater than their own. Humbly sharing the Master's experience they too say, I have overcome the world, and with them, as with him, that victory springs from more than pluck, more than a philosophy of life only; it springs from an actual working alliance with a source of power from beyond themselves.

This is rather a frightening generation in which to live. The war has been won for a year now, but look at the world! A physician, we are told, said recently to one of his patients, "What you need is a few months vacation on another planet." I'll say so! But we cannot get it. It is here, with our personal difficulties and with a desperately troubled era on our hands, that we must win our inward victory. And that calls for an experience which, as Dr. Moffatt translates the words, Paul described as "a mighty increase of strength by his Spirit in the inner man."

Some lives here are going to crack up unless they find that kind of religion, a religion that actually works, God to them no theory just, but energy, power, that they can tap. This man, for example, faced an impossible situation; his troubles were more than anyone could be expected to endure; they towered above him until fear, that Svengali of the soul, began hypnotizing him, saying, You cannot take it, you are going to crack up. Well, he thought he would, until, remembering some things he had heard, he turned within, and as a last desperate resource went far down where the deep springs of the spirit touch the nether wells, and lo! something happened. As really as in a scientific laboratory an experiment works, this worked. When far within he reached out for power, he touched, not nothing but something. So he did not crack up but turned that most difficult crisis into spiritual victory, and neither he nor his religion has been the same since. Were you to talk with him about it he would say, Man, this Christian religion actually works!

How we need that experience today! The thing I fear most for folk like ourselves is that we should do what Henry Adams did. Henry Adams came from one of our great American families, with heritage, fortune, prestige, education, all outward circumstances in his favor. But he did not like this pitiful world, this violent, contemptible human race, and he derided the whole paltry scheme. As his biographer says, "It was easier to sit back and proclaim life unworthy of Henry Adams than it was to lean forward with the whole soul in a passionate, if inadequate, effort to make Henry Adams worthy of life." Such cynicism as Henry Adams retreated to is more than easy now. It lets a man sit back, saying that the world is not worthy of him, when he ought to be girding himself to make his life worthy to meet the challenge of the world. Millions of our fellowmen are crushed by circumstance that nobody can stand up against. You cannot build a triumphant soul on starvation. That is asking too much. All the more reason, then, why we who are not hungry, who are not hopelessly overborne by circumstance should surmount life and carry off the victory in the face of it. And more than pluck is needed to do that; more than just a philosophy believed with the mind; an inner experience of power is needed from beyond ourselves that makes us adequate for life.

I had rather hear my friend, the founder of Alcoholics Anonymous, talk about God than any theologian I know. A militant agnostic, scornful of religion, he was hopelessly beaten by drink, and then, to his amazement, reaching out in his despair for some power to save him, he found it. You should hear him talk about God—humbly, no theological dogmatism in him, not thinking he knows much about God, but sure, absolutely sure, of one thing: a Power is here greater than ourselves that we can get in touch with and that can give to man spiritual mastery over life.

Such a man really believes in God, and not even a dismaying era like this will whip him. General MacArthur said the other day, "Nobody can stop the irresistible influence of a sound idea." Walk around that statement and consider it well! If that is true, then this cannot be merely a materialistic universe. It is nonsense to suppose that in a merely materialistic universe nothing can stop the irresistible influence of a sound idea. A spiritual Power must be operative in any world where that is true.

Does not the story of our Lord confirm this? His family called him "beside himself," his church thought him a heretic, his nation's rulers regarded him as a public menace to be liquidated, he was betrayed by his friend and crucified by his government. But what General MacArthur says was true of him. His ideas lived; no nail pierced them, no sepulchre entombed them; he was allied with a Power stronger than all the mighty things that withstood him. To see that fact about life, to experience it even a little—that's really believing in God!

Our message sums up in this—don't let the objective facts get you down! It is still man's subjective contribution, his pluck and courage, his great philosophies of life, his alliance with the unseen powers of the spiritual world, that determine the issue. If we are personally whipped, not external circumstances so much as our inner breakdown causes our collapse. It is a great day in a man's experience when he makes up his mind that within himself, under his control, are the forces that can make his life victorious. So Edna St. Vincent Millay says it:

> "The world stands out on either side
> No wider than the heart is wide;
> Above the world is stretched the sky,—
> No higher than the soul is high.
> The heart can push the sea and land
> Farther away on either hand;
> The soul can split the sky in two,
> And let the face of God shine through.
> But East and West will pinch the heart
> That cannot keep them pushed apart;
> And he whose soul is flat—the sky
> Will cave in on him by and by."

People Who Suppose
They Have No Personal Relationships with God

EVERY counselor meets people unaware that they have any personal relationship with God. Some of them disbelieve in God; some are agnostic about God; but even if theoretically they believe in him they are unconscious of any personal dealings with him. Now from the Christian point of view that is impossible. Granting that God is, he is, of course, an omnipresent, inescapable fact; a man can no more avoid dealing with him than a man can live in a physical universe, made up of protons and electrons, and not deal with them. He may be ignorant about them and unaware of them, but he certainly deals with them all the time.

Many people have such unrecognized relationships with God. Some time since a man accosted me saying that he regularly listened to the radio sermons on Sunday afternoon but that as for himself he had no religion. Nothing was going on inside him, he said, that suggested God. Before we were through talking, however, he had to admit realms in his life where he did deal with a power greater than himself, whom he could no more avoid having relationships with than a dweller in a solar system can avoid relationships with the sun.

Parting from him I quoted a verse of Isaiah's where the prophet pictures God saying to Cyrus the Persian, "I girded thee, though thou hast not known me." Cyrus was King of Babylon; he was a polytheist; in one inscription which we still have he professes himself a devotee of Bel-Merodack and Nebo, Babylonian deities. He knew little or nothing about Israel's God, acknowledged no relationships with him or obligations to him. None the less, Israel's God said to him, "I girded thee, though thou hast not known me."

On Being Fit To Live With

How familiar an experience it is to be ministered to by forces we do not recognize! That experience began in the womb. Every mother can say to her new-born babe, I girded thee, though thou hast not known me. So Addison's hymn put it ·

> "Unnumbered comforts to my soul
> Thy tender care bestow'd,
> Before my infant heart conceiv'd
> From whom those comforts flow'd."

We commonly suppose ourselves served only by forces we know about and consciously acknowledge, but our lives are constantly enriched by ministries we are unaware of or utterly misconceive.

During long ages man did not understand the physical universe, but still the sun warmed him, the rain refreshed him, the returning seasons fed him and the stars guided his wandering boats. Illustrations of this experience—being ministered to from misconceived and unrecognized sources—come thick and fast. A young child does not see that he is undergirded by his country's institutions, unaware even that there is a Constitution of the United States or a Bill of Rights; but later the national life that has long given him security begins saying to him, I girded thee, though thou hast not known me.

Surely this truth applies to our relationships with God. Some people seem to think that God does not enter into a man's life, liberate him, guide him, employ him to noble ends, unless God is consciously recognized and received. But the God of the Bible does not so behave. Rather like the sun he comes in through every crack and crevice where he can find a way. Through any door or window left unwittingly ajar where he can steal, though unobserved, to lift and liberate a life, the God of the Bible enters in. With many a fine man, therefore, who says he disbelieves in God, God has been dealing, even using him, it may be, as he did Cyrus, for great ends saying, "I girded thee, though thou hast not known me." Someone here today should feel that true about himself.

Consider the explanation this provides for some fine characters we know. Cyrus played a creative part in his time. In his release of captive nations in Babylon, he ended one of his generation's most grievous wrongs and, helping to re-establish the exiled Jewish community on Mt. Zion, he made a contribution to history to which we are all indebted. Yet he did not know God. Cyrus is a symbol of some people who often perplex us, high-minded, useful lives who do not recognize God.

You know what some religious folks say about them. They call Cyrus names—agnostic, infidel, atheist. They imply that God has nothing to do with the moral quality or public service of a good man who does not consciously acknowledge him. I cannot credit that. I know some of these Cyruses too well.

Some of our great scientists belong in this group. While today we comfortably worship here, in many an obscure laboratory they seek cures for ancient lamentable ills and, finding them, will make it a point of honor, without profit to themselves, to share their knowledge with the world. Let the preachers stop quarreling with such scientists and emulate a little, if they can, their disinterested love of truth and their unselfish service. But some of them do not recognize God.

So it is with some philanthropists. While too many so-called Christians make of their religion an emotional retreat into a make-believe world of personal comfort for themselves, these philanthropic soldiers of the common good are out in the real world, fighting real foes—poverty, unemployment, the inhumanities of our economic life and the insanities of war. They are great spirits; our children will rise up to call them blessed. But some of them do not recognize God.

What shall we say about such folk? Some people use such scientists and philanthropists as arguments against religion. See, they say, these splendid men and women living without God! But they are not living without God. They are supreme examples of the unrecognized God. Listen to the New Testament: "He that doeth good is of God." And again, says the New Testament, "He that abideth in love abideth in God, and God abideth in him." There in the service he renders, in the love that motives him, in the mission that has mastered him, *is* God, girding him, even though unknown.

Some time ago in the small hours of the morning I walked up and down Broadway with one of the leading citizens of this community. His dominant passion is to be of use, and because his character is unblemished and his ability great the scope of his service far overpasses the range of most of us. Amid the restless crowds and glaring lights of Broadway we walked, talking about God. He was not irreverent, but he could not believe. He wistfully wished he could, but for himself he could see nothing except to be agnostic and to live a serviceable life until he fell on sleep. All the way home that night, after I left my friend, I kept thinking of some other people I know. Here is one who does believe in God. Brought up to believe in God, he has never faced the mystery and misery of life sympathetically enough to have his faith disturbed. I compared him with my friend who could not believe, for he, with deep emotion, had talked about the miseries of men—multitudes starving; the poor, whose existence is a long animal struggle to keep the body alive; the sufferings that fall with such terrific incidence upon the vast, obscure, forgotten masses of mankind—and out of the very ardor of his humane sympathy had cried, How can you believe that a good God made the world like this?

Now I believe in God. But the God I believe in likes that man! I think Jesus would estimate him far higher than the other man, who never had been so disturbed by life's miseries as to be troubled in his faith. Whenever, therefore, I meet Cyrus, in Babylon or on Broadway, I am glad that there is something in the Bible about him except condemnation. I rejoice, as Isaiah did, to hear the living God saying to him, as Dr. Moffatt translates our text: "You know me not, but I delight in you."

Turn now to ourselves, and see where this truth comes home to us. When any man tells me that he has no personal dealings with God, I feel sure he is mistaken. Oh, for example, in the moral realm! Someone here has come so close to going to pieces in moral dishonor—financial, sexual, what you will—that you do not yet understand why you did not go to pieces. There, on the verge of the precipice you stood and something held you back—a face rose before you, a hand held you, so that you did not fall, and here you are today with some disgraceful things undone. Something at the heart of your life has presented to temptation's appeal a resistance that surprised you. Some people say that it is easy to sin. That is not the whole truth. We all know what they mean, but still it is not the whole truth. It is not easy to sin. Deep in all of us there is something we have to fight against and trample on and blind ourselves to and desperately struggle to forget, before we are free to sin. You do not believe in God? Where do you think God is? Just among the stars? There at the center of your life, the patient guardian of your honor, is the real God. Many a year he has been trying to make some of us hear his voice and recognize it: "I girded thee, though thou hast not known me."

Or, again, many of us have tried to give up God, and have never quite succeeded. We say there is no God and then we go out under the stars at night, and wonder. A vast, law-abiding universe this, to have come by accident, as though a man should throw a font of type upon the floor and by chance it should arrange itself into a play of Shakespeare. Strange universe, without God! We say there is no God and then we pick up some great biography and wonder. In a merely materialistic world it is strange that spiritual life should rise to such heights—all this ethical struggle and achievement but a passing spark, struck off as it were by falling stones in a merely physical world. Strange universe, without God! Or we try to say there is no God and then we are married, and the first baby comes, and there wells up in us the purest love that human beings know, the love of parents for a little child. Queer business, for a man to walk about the streets with a love like that in his heart, trying to think that there is nothing corresponding with it in the reality from which the man's heart and the man's home came. Strange universe, without God! Or we try to say there is no God and then we grow old, and some we most have loved pass away, as Carlyle said his mother did, like "the last pale sickle of the moon, . . . sinking in the dark seas." Queer, to think that souls like that are completely at the mercy of a few particles of disordered matter. Strange universe, without God!

We have never succeeded in getting rid of God. There is a flame in our heart that will not go out. Friends, if there were no God it would be easier to disbelieve in him than it is! We cannot get rid of God, because all that is best in us *is* God in us. The flame is he, and there in the center of our life for many a year he has been trying to make us hear, "I girded thee, though thou hast not known me."

Indeed, our thought carries us farther. Not individuals alone but mankind as a whole neglects and forgets God. Yet because of that does God lose his hold upon the reins of human destiny? Rather, there is a power greater than ourselves that, recognized or not, goes on its everlasting way. Sometimes I come alone into the church just to see the cross over the altar. It is strange that it should be there. That cross stands for one of the darkest deeds in history. What worse thing can be said about this world than that it is the kind of place where that could happen—so glorious a person done to so cruel and shameful a death. So, long ago, Pilate sat in judgment upon Jesus, but not now! Now Jesus sits in judgment on Pilate. Long ago, his judges condemned Socrates, but not now! Now Socrates condemns his judges. Long ago, the inquisitors tried Galileo, but not now! Now Galileo tries his inquisitors. There is an everlasting fact beneath the aphorisms of the race: "No lie can last forever"; "Truth will out"; "Truth crushed to earth will rise again"; "He laughs best who laughs last." Say our worst about this world, it is indeed a place where many a violent dictator has laughed, but where no dictator ever laughs last. Within the shadow, recognized or not, often neglected, forgotten, betrayed, the Power not ourselves that makes for righteousness has said to man, "I girded thee, though thou hast not known me."

What, then, is the conclusion of the matter? That we ought to be contented to go through a long life ministered to by an unrecognized God? Upon the contrary, this sermon has been preached in vain if all the way through you have not felt the pity of being served by the Eternal Spirit of all grace, and still not knowing him.

The central experience in man's personal relationship with God is prayer. Now I contend that everybody prays. Call it by what different names they may, all men pray. For a man to say he never prays is as if a man should say that he never responds to nature's beauty. Were one to say that, we would be incredulous. What! we would cry, you never love beauty in nature? Never? Not when you see white birch trees against green backgrounds, not when you see sunsets in the mountains, or hear

> " . . . a hidden brook
> In the leafy month of June,
> That to the sleeping woods all night
> Singeth a quiet tune"?

And one would feel sure that even though Central Park represented the limit of opportunity, we would find somewhere, somehow, in every man, a capacity to respond to natural beauty.

Well, praying is as universal as that. Not by aggressive activity alone does any one of us achieve all that he inwardly possesses or lives by. In receptive hours rather, when we are hospitable to something higher than ourselves, we are enriched. Every soul knows that. Of course we pray—sometimes, to be sure, unwittingly, as though a man by accident left the door of

his spirit open and some God-like idea or feeling strayed in—
but sometimes consciously, experiencing a divine invasion that
is unmistakable. To go into the woods, as Sidney Lanier said of
Jesus in Gethsemane, "clean forspent, forspent," and there, com-
muning with a Presence higher than ourselves, to achieve an
inward victory, so that,

> "Out of the woods my Master went,
> And He was well content"—

something like that experience we do know. Of course we pray!
Dr. Jacks of England described a friend of his, a shoemaker, in
words that apply to some people I know: "He spent his breath
in proving that God did not exist, but spent his life in proving
that He did." Friend, you do have dealings with God. Stop calling that experience by another name, and recognize it for what
it is.

One of the most charming stories of the last generation was
Jean Webster's *Daddy Long Legs*. Many of you will recall the
gist of the tale, how a young girl in an orphanage was befriended
by a person whom she did not know. He took a fancy to her
when she was a very little child and befriended her, keeping
himself unknown. Year after year the favors flowed in upon her
from her unknown friend. She grew up through girlhood and
young college womanhood, her opportunities provided by this
friend she did not know. Once she saw him but she did not
recognize him. She had imagined him looking other than he did
look and so even when she saw him she did not know him.
What if the story ended there? Why, what a way to end a story
—served through long years by a friend and then not knowing
him! No! She found him out at last and loved him, her long unrecognized benefactor. I beg of you, do not let your life story end
without that consummation!

Now, in this closing moment, to some soul here does not a
voice out of the unseen come: I have been girding thee, though
thou hast not known me, whom to know aright is life eternal.

On Being Only a Drop in the Bucket

THE story of Jesus feeding five thousand people with a few loaves and fishes, raises questions in a modern mind. Similar stories are not unfamiliar in the ancient world, and one something like it is told of Gautama Buddha. Many guesses have been made as to what actually happened and naturalistic explanations have been offered, such as, for example, that starting with one boy's few loaves and fishes, it turned out in the end that when all the people pooled the food they had brought and distributed it fairly, the crowd had plenty and to spare. Interpret the scene in your own way. In this sermon we are dealing with one character, whose attitude, whatever one's explanation of the story as a whole may be, brings him very close to us. When Jesus suggested to the disciples that they feed the multitude, Andrew looked at the Master incredulously, saying, "There is a boy here with five barley loaves and a couple of fish; but what is that among so many?"

If Andrew felt that, how do you suppose the boy himself felt? The need of that assemblage made his individual resources seem useless. What could he do? Look at the size of the problem, and then look at his five barley loaves and a couple of fish, futile to solve the multitude's predicament! He was only a drop in the bucket.

Such individual futility is one of the major trials we face today. We look at mankind, convulsed with the consequences of total war, involving such vast and ominous catastrophe as makes the ablest statesmen, for all their show window speeches, shake in their shoes, and then we look at ourselves, one by one. What can we do? The world's calamity, we feel, is like an earthquake; we are lucky if personally we keep our stance; as for stopping it, or preventing the recurrence of it, what can we individually do?

[176]

Difficulty can be stimulating, arousing in us character and effort that easy days do not call out, but to produce that effect there must be some relevance and proportion between the size of the problem and our ability and resource. Today, however, this global disaster for many of us has gone far beyond the stimulating point. The scope of it is so vast, the factors determining what will come of it so far beyond our individual control, that as we face it we feel, not stimulation, but personal futility and helplessness.

To be sure, day after day we go on, trying to do our part as good citizens, but that is no answer to the deeper problem. Behind our busyness in the immediate emergency, we wonder what kind of world will come of it for our children, in what worth-while or utterly vain consequence the terrific sacrifices of this generation will issue. What Stalin decides may shape the future of mankind, and what can you and I do about it, or about any of these global determinants of destiny upon whose tidal flow we float like chips? No one here altogether avoids that mood of baffled futility, or fails to hear its echoes in others, as though each of us, looking at himself, were saying, A boy with five barley loaves and a couple of fish, but what is that among so many?

Nevertheless, that boy has gone down in history, a result coming from his slender lunch that has been worth remembering. Perhaps he illustrates something everlastingly true about the importance of individuals in the face of massive problems.

For one thing, it is clearly true that in the long run everything good or bad in the world depends on the quality of individuals. This war itself was the vastest global enterprise of its kind man ever undertook, and yet daily we were assailed by appeals to us as individuals. The home front as important as the battle front, all of us were talked to as though the whole business might bog down if, one by one, we did not stand by. Moreover, those pleas came from hardheaded realists, who would have wasted no time appealing to us so, with our five barley loaves and a couple of fish, if they had not really thought we mattered. If the individual counts so critically in global war, why not in global peace?

What common men and women think, do and are today, does matter. As Albert Edward Wiggam, one of the least sentimental of writers on social questions, said, "If hope and courage go out of the lives of common men it is all up with social and political civilization." Thus to stress our importance, one by one, is no mere psychological shot-in-the-arm to buck us up, but a serious public matter. To be sure, to the Christian minister this theme is doubtless first suggested by the desire to help some people rise above the sense of futile worthlessness, one of the most dilapidated moods afflicting personality, but when one gets into it one finds himself dealing, not with personal encouragement alone, but with serious realistic facts. We say the ancient Greeks condemned Socrates to death, but it was not so simple as that. On the jury that condemned Socrates were 501 men; 281 of them voted for his death, 220 for his acquittal. There is a true parable of history's crises. If only some individuals had changed their minds, what crimes could have been avoided, and what gains made!

Once at a wayside lunchroom a friend of mine found himself seated next to Will Rogers, the comedian, and in the course of conversation said, "What's wrong with the world, anyway?" To which Will Rogers drawled in answer, "Well, I dunno. I guess it's people." I guess it is! The evils of the world are massive, but only when we break down the massiveness into its individual components do we get at the heart of the matter. We cannot build a great cathedral out of loose sandstone. Today our eyes are naturally centered on vast structures of world organization, but what the political architects can do in rearing them depends ultimately on the material they have to build with, and that material, in the last analysis, is inside individuals. One by one, we do count! As Archbishop Temple of Canterbury put it, "No statesmanship can ensure peace in a world where men, as individuals and as citizens, are selfish in their outlook and grasping in their conduct."

The truth we are dealing with gains force when we note that each of us is more than a mere individual; he is an individual, plus the ideas he stands for. A slender wire can carry a strong current; a small window can let in a lot of light; and an ordinary man can stand for ideas on which the world's salvation depends.

One of the marvels of history is the way mankind's great gains have started. An idea gets hold of an individual; commonly not in himself a notable personality, he feels shocked and humbled at the disproportion between himself and the idea that gains possession of him, saying, like Isaiah, "I am a man of unclean lips, and I dwell in the midst of a people of unclean lips," or like Jeremiah, "Ah, Lord God! behold, I cannot speak: for I am a child." Nevertheless, that extraordinary idea for which even an ordinary man can stand, possesses him, and when he stands for it he becomes more than himself, as a window is more than itself when the sun shines through. Thus mankind's major gains always start, and then the saving idea goes out into the world, appealing to persons one by one, saying, Believe in me, stand for me; and when enough individuals have believed it and become its representatives, it overrides all the opposition man's ignorance and sin can rear against it. All man's intellectual and moral triumphs have so been won, and far from making the individual peripheral, this fact makes him central.

Today, some of the most important ideas mankind ever faced are thus asking for the use of our personal influence. That we ourselves, one by one, do not amount to much is true, but the ideas we can stand for are crucial. A world organized for peace, a world free from the curse of racial prejudice, from the arrogance of master races and imperialistic nations, free from the fear of war, free from bigotry, intolerance and hate, men and nations fit to live with and moving out toward a day of co-operation for the good of all—such ideas are here, they have started, they are on their way, and they are mankind's hope. To say simply that their realization depends on the world's political organization will not do. Of course, it depends on that! But that, in turn, depends on enough ordinary, average people, like you and me, who deeply, tirelessly, undiscourageably, believe in those ideas and stand for them.

In contrast with this attitude, our debilitating sense of individual futility stands out as the tragedy it is. It would be a tragedy if it meant only that one man in an age like this, looking at his five barley loaves and a couple of fish, retreated to a discouraged mood of personal uselessness, and did nothing. But a man who thus feels his individual uselessness commonly goes farther, and thinking hopelessly that he can do nothing, generalizes his sense of helplessness and concludes that nothing can be done at all. One of our fighting men, fed up with the whole business, his own sense of personal futility generalized into discouragement about mankind's possibilities, said recently to a friend of mine, "After the war I'll give the world one more chance. If it goes on being a mess like this, to hell with it! I'll go listen to good music." If enough individuals take that attitude, then we are done for!

In 1828 a debate was held at Harvard University as to whether it would ever be possible for one presidential administration to extend from the Atlantic to the Pacific, and they decided that that was inconceivable. If today we have a continental nation, that achievement is indeed the result of large-scale political organization, but behind that have been millions of individuals who have believed in the United States through thick and thin, ordinary folk, standing for an idea that despite towering difficulties has come true.

Thomas Jefferson in his day said something about Americans that one prays may be true now. Had it not been true then, we would not be here. "It is," said Jefferson, "part of the American character to consider nothing as desperate." Whether or not that is part of the American character, it ought to be part of the Christian character. See what might easily have happened to that boy with his loaves and fishes! The disproportion between the size of the problem and the meagerness of his resources made him feel at first a mere spectator, tempted to do nothing but watch the unrolling of events among the multitude, just as we are tempted now to stand off and watch this war torn world as a vast spectacle. Then Christ, to his amazement, changed him from a spectator to a participant. He did matter. His loaves and fishes counted. He was no longer on the side lines watching, but in the center of the game. Give us enough individuals in whom Christ has wrought that change, standing each in his own place for the saving ideas that challenge the world today, and their achievement is not impossible.

If ever in history men needed that lesson, those first disciples did. They themselves did not amount to much. What could that small group of fishermen and the like do against the stupendous evil of the world and the towering might of the Roman Empire? Every man of them must have put himself into the place of that boy—five barley loaves and a couple of fish; but what is that among so many? Yet Christ did something with them, incredible, miraculous, in comparison with which the feeding of the five thousand pales into insignificance.

Why God so works his consequences out, no mortal mind can tell, but this is the way he works, even in the physical realm. The most prolific, edible grains mankind depends on today are varieties that stem out from Marquis wheat, millions upon millions of bushels raised now in North America, and used to feed ourselves and the world, but just forty years ago all the Marquis wheat in existence could have been put into one envelope. Less than a boy's lunch has been multiplied to feed an innumerable multitude.

As for the spiritual realm, why God so works we may not understand, but how he does it we can see. For an individual is more than an individual, not only because he can stand for ideas greater than himself, but because he is, as it were, a ganglion in the nervous system of humanity. "None of us liveth to himself," says the New Testament. You and I are joined together by vital nerves of intercommunication, and each of us, so linked, is joined to others still, and they to others, so that what I think, and am, and stand for, spreads to them, every impulse that any ganglion imparts affecting at last the whole nervous system of humanity.

Even in the days of isolated nations and races this was true; the nervous system of personal relationships encompassed the globe, and through it what was thought, believed and done anywhere, at last reached everywhere. So James Russell Lowell sang:

"When a deed is done for Freedom, through the broad
        earth's aching breast
Runs a thrill of joy prophetic, trembling on from east
        to west, . . .
For mankind are one in spirit, and an instinct bears
        along,
Round the earth's electric circle, the swift flash of right
        or wrong."

That was true even when Lowell said it, but now our new world of interlacing communications accentuates its truth. Is it nothing to us what the common people of Russia, China, Britain, France, India, one by one, are thinking? Nothing matters much more. The emergence in our time of institutions like the Gallup poll is no accident; we want to know what the people are thinking—not big people but little people, average people, for in the long run everything depends on that. We commonly think of what Mr. Willkie called *One World* as arguing only the necessity of vast, over-all global organization, but it means more than that. This new interdependence of mankind accentuates, to a degree never known in history before, the importance of what, one by one, we think and are. Every individual starts a ripple that soon or late reaches the farthest shore.

To be sure, it takes imagination to see this. Let a man view himself as a single item confronting the turbulent world and he may easily feel discouraged, as Nathaniel Hawthorne did under the strain of the Civil War: "The present, the immediate and the actual have proved too potent for me." What difference do I make, he is tempted to think; I am a mere individual; I am only an atom—but at that point I should suppose he would stop short. That is just what he is, an atom, and everything depends now on the release of the spiritual energy in just such atoms.

The right kind of individual, for example, is manifestly necessary in creating a good home. But, as Christ came from the Holy Family in Nazareth, so the center of the world's redemption is always in the home. Our Christian ideal for the world is to make a family of it, where the fatherhood of God is fulfilled in the brotherhood of man, every personality valued for its own sake, as in a good family, and all together living in friendship and good will. If that ideal is to come true for the world, it must be more and more true in more and more families. Homes are greenhouses where all growth starts, that, transplanted to mankind's larger relationships, can make the whole earth fair. Whoever helps build a good home is in so far furnishing indispensable material for the building of a good world.

A returning soldier thus described to a friend what meant most to him when he came back: "One has gripped my hand and said a bit huskily, 'Well, son—Oh son, but it's good to see you!' One has held me in her arms and cried a bit and seen that I had my favorite dessert after dinner. One has said and done a number of things that are nobody's business but hers and mine. One has put muddy paws on my uniform and nearly wagged his tail off trying to tell me that he's glad to see me." God forgive us if we ever let the dust gather on these simple, humble, home relationships! For here is the affirmation of

Christian faith: I believe in the home; I believe in it so much that I see in it the eternal truth about God and man; I believe that in the relationships of a good home are the foretaste and prophecy of a redeemed world; and that, though battles rage and empires rise and fall, over the Holy Family God's star still stands and his angels sing. Every individual, therefore, helping to make a good home, matters to the whole world.

Beyond these inner groups, however, on which our personal influence directly plays, we can add our small strength to the right side of the world's major issues. During the first World War I preached one Sunday in Inverness, Scotland. It was one of the darkest days of the conflict; a great offensive was on; Scotch regiments were in the thick of it, and that congregation knew their menfolk that morning were falling at the front. The nearest I ever came to losing control of myself in the pulpit was when that overflowing congregation sang from their Scotch psalter until the building fairly rocked:

> "God is our refuge and our strength,
> In straits a present aid.
> Therefore, although the earth be moved
> We will not be afraid."

Why is it that in war men and women rise to such heights of faith, courage and steadfast loyalty, and then in peacetime flatten out, as so many of us do? Every individual there that morning knew that he counted.

Five barley loaves and a couple of fish; but what is that among so many?—that is not the last word, not in a world where God still works, as Jesus said, through the leaven in the meal. Ah, Christ, still calling commonplace fishermen from their nets, and counting in the end on getting enough of them to change the world, call us today, and let no appalling contrast between the size of the world's problems and the littleness of our resources blind our eyes to the fact that forever and forever the individual matters—the soul of all reformation the reformation of the soul!

Christ Himself Is Christianity *

THIS Christmas season finds us a rather bewildered human race, facing a confused world, man's wild behavior dangerously out of control. No neat formula from anywhere can solve our problems or allay our anxiety, but today we turn to one man in the New Testament who lived in an age not unlike our own, and who carried on with hope and confidence. He wrote the letter to the Hebrews. In his time, too, the world was shaken. Within the confines of the Roman Empire nations, races, religions, economies had been poured into the artificial unity of one world before men were ready for one world. Confusion reigned, and as for his own people, only a few years before he wrote Jerusalem had been laid waste, the Holy Land desolate, its population slain or scattered. Over his world, too, man had not been able to establish intelligent, ethical control, and in that situation, as Dr. Moffatt translates it, he wrote in his second chapter: "As it is, we do not yet see all things controlled by man; what we do see is Jesus."

That text seems made for us this Christmas season. The writer was thinking of an old psalm—

"What is man, that thou art mindful of him?
or the son of man, that thou carest for him?"—

a psalm which describes God's purpose, crowning man at last with glory and honor and putting all things in subjection under his feet, establishing, that is, man's intelligent, ethical control over the world. Well, says this writer, we are a long way from that; we do not yet see all things controlled by man; but with that negative statement he does not stop. He adds the affirmative factor that for him changes the whole perspective of his outlook: "What we do see is Jesus."

* A Christmas Sermon.

[185]

In saying this the writer was not turning from realistic facts to a beautiful ideal; he was turning from one set of facts to another fact. Jesus, too, was a fact. He had actually come. That life had been lived. If we are to base our lives on facts, must we not take that fact in too? As this writer saw him, Christ was a towering, challenging, revealing fact, and to see him changed his whole outlook on life. On the threshold of our Christmas season we try today to share that experience.

Let us start by saying that Jesus' coming was a prophetic fact. Once on all this planet there was just one form of life, one-celled creatures in the slime along the ocean's edge, but looking back on that so small beginning we see it now as a prophetic fact. Once there was the first emergence of what could be called a human mind, putting two and two together and drawing conclusions from premises, but dim as that dawning intelligence was, it was a prophetic fact. Once, about five thousand years before Christ, there first appeared on earth what could be called a social conscience, its earliest expressions still readable in Egypt's ancient literature, but hesitant and uncertain as that social conscience was, who can measure the significance of that prophetic fact? Once everybody thought the sun revolved about the earth, and then Copernicus came, and in one mind and those it influenced there dawned a new way of thinking, and that was a prophetic fact.

This is the way the world runs. Always the new beginnings to which the future belongs are born, as it were, in a manger, their prophetic import seen by none save three wise men, it may be, and a few shepherds. So in every generation, in some realm or other, there is always some Bethlehem in which amid the world's darkness a new light shines, with few to notice and fewer yet to believe, and yet there is the ·great prophetic fact of that generation and, it may be, of all future time.

Thus the writer to the Hebrews saw Jesus—not chiefly as a beautiful ideal. In Christ's coming he saw something tremendous happening in the world, the emergence of a prophetic fact that would outlast all the mighty things that withstood it. In this very paragraph where our text is found, the writer calls Jesus "the Pioneer" of our salvation. So to him too the world was wild, uncivilized, uncontrolled, but at least this much had happened—the trail blazer had come. Is not that the way everything worth while starts? Once there was no scientific medicine—but then Pasteur; once there was no competent nursing for the sick—but then, Florence Nightingale; once there was no religious liberty free from the State's regimentation—but then, Roger Williams. To all such cases at the start our text applied: we do not yet see all things brought under control. Far from it! But we do see the pioneer. At least he has come; the movement he represents has begun; that much has happened. Such confidence about Christ this Christmas chiefly means to me.

In this congregation today there must be much hidden pessimism concerning the possibility of man's intelligent, ethical control over this world, and when the lovely stories of the Christ child are retold, in all the sentimental beauty with which Christmas clothes them, that may only make the stark realities seem starker yet. It takes more faith than I have, a man may say, to believe in the triumph of Christ's way of life in such a world. To which I answer: in all these cases we have just rehearsed, the crux of the matter was not simply faith, but intelligence and insight. It takes intelligence and insight to recognize, at first, Copernicus and Pasteur and Florence Nightingale and Roger Williams and all the rest for what they really are—prophetic facts to which the future belongs. For that I plead today in our thought of Christ. He is the Pioneer; he has begun a new way of life. All things brought under man's control we do not yet see but this much has happened—the trail blazer has arrived. That is something. "What we do see is Jesus."

Moreover the coming of Jesus was not only a prophetic but a momentously influential fact. We have been living through a generation when the determining influences in human history have been more and more defined in impersonal terms. Heredity, that settles everything; economic determinism, that settles everything—such has been the strong trend in our generation's thinking. You students at the University know how far this has gone, some saying that geography and climate account for almost all our human story; some, like the Marxians, that economic determinism is the explanation; some, like Veblen, that technical developments, such as machine industry, are the really determinative factors; and always the exponents of heredity saying that it is our genes that predestinate us all to be what we are. So, in a world discouraging enough already, this powerful emphasis on the impersonal factors predetermining our destiny has made personality seem a helpless by-product and mere victim of the impersonal.

And now Christmas comes again with its ringing announcement of a personality who splits history into B.C. and A.D. That message we critically need. There have been times when Christmas could be merely sweet.

> "The Christ Child stood at Mary's knee
> His hair was like a crown;
> And all the flowers looked up at him
> And all the stars looked down."

God grant us all a taste of that poetic, lovely side of Christmas in our homes this year! But the full meaning of Christ's coming goes far, far deeper. Into a world where all the deterministic factors men enlarge upon today were in full force and effect, a child was born under the humblest of conditions in a conquered province of the Roman Empire, and in some thirty years only, of which only a few months were spent in public ministry, had his chance to say his say and reveal his quality. And to multitudes he has changed the whole complexion of the world.

There must be something to be said for the proposition that it is personality, too, that shapes the course of history. We cannot tell the story of music, or art, or science, or ethics, or philosophy, or religion, and leave creative personality out. The coming of a great person is the most influential event in history.

So, once more, our text comes true: "As it is, we do not yet see all things controlled by man; what we do see is Jesus." To be able to say that today, nearly two thousand years after Jesus' birth, is astounding. What chance had he to survive? Were not all the impersonal factors against him? And as for man, man tried hard enough to get rid of him. Herod tried it, slaughtering the innocents in Bethlehem. Pilate thought he had done it, on Calvary. And ever since, by every device that disbelief and wickedness can use, men have endeavored to be rid of him. But here he is still. This changing, shifting, wayward, brutal world can get rid of a lot of things—but not of a personality like that.

Early in this last war a member of the British Parliament in public debate exclaimed, "God help the British Empire if it must be defended by the ethics of the Sermon on the Mount!" One can easily understand his feeling that. But now the war has been fought, and modern war's true nature has been lighted up with such lurid horror as leaves the whole world stunned, and the atomic bomb has come, and today everyone with any sense is saying, God help the British Empire and all the rest of us if we go on with this process generation after generation! Ah, Christ of God, we cannot get rid of you. Whenever we seriously seek the world's salvation, we come back to you. You are not just a beautiful ideal; you are the most persistent, inescapable, and in the long run influential figure that ever entered human history.

Now let us bring what we have been saying closer home to our private lives. The coming of Jesus, more than a prophetic and influential fact in history, is a profoundly moving fact in personal experience. It is not abstractions but persons who most deeply influence us.

The organ in this church is dedicated to William Newton Clarke. When I was an undergraduate in college he was a professor in the graduate department in the university. I was having a perplexing time with my religion then. I had thrown almost all of it overboard. During my sophomore year wild horses could hardly have dragged me inside a church. I started out for my junior year telling my family that I was going to clear God out of the universe and begin all over to see what I could find. But there, walking across the campus, was William Newton Clarke. He knew more about modern thinking than I began to know; yet there he was, a Christian, an intelligent, forward-looking, intellectually honest Christian. His very presence seemed to say: Essential Christianity is not irreconcilable with modern knowledge; he who is afraid to face facts does not really believe in God; come, the truth shall make you free. I have had a grand time in the ministry these forty years and more, but I am sure it was not geography or climate, economic determinism or technological industry that put me there. It was a person—William Newton Clarke—who opened the door.

What is the most moving force in our experience as we sit here? People—some of them still with us, some of them passed into the unseen. What most helps us to keep straight when we dreadfully want to go crooked, or steady when we are tempted to crack up? The love, the example, the persuasiveness of some people. What is it that most of all would utterly wreck our lives? To have some people let us down. Not abstractions but persons most deeply determine our lives.

To be sure, this is more apparent in some realms than in others. Someone here may already have been thinking, Why cannot religion do in this regard what science does? Science makes no such fuss as religion does over its pioneering personalities; science abstracts the ideas of Darwin, uses the valid, discards the residue and moves on; but the pioneers themselves, while honored, play no such part in the thought of science as Christ plays in the adoration of Christianity. To which I answer, You are quite right; in this regard, there is a difference between science on one side, and, on the other, such realms as art, music, morals, love, religion. We can abstract the ideas of Darwin and forget Darwin himself. But, friends, we never can abstract the art of Toscanini from Toscanini; Toscanini's art *is* Toscanini. We never can abstract the lover's love from the lover, keeping it and forgetting him; the lover's love is the lover. We never can abstract the quality of Jesus from Jesus, and forget him; Jesus' quality is Jesus. Science may be made a realm of abstract propositions, but religion is a realm of personal, spiritual values which always must be incarnate to be seen and understood. If it is to be real, the word must become flesh and dwell among us. So William James when asked to define what he meant by the word "spirituality" hesitated, and then said he was not sure he could put into words what he thought spirituality meant, but he could point to a person who was it—Phillips Brooks.

Thus to the writer of the letter to the Hebrews Christ himself is Christianity. Ask him what the persistent, eternal factor in Christianity is, and he will offer no abstract theology in answer; he knows that theology is changeable; he says, "Jesus Christ . . . the same, yesterday, to-day, and for ever." Ask him what it means ethically to live a Christian life and he gives no abstract code of moral laws; he knows that moral customs alter; he says, "Consider the Apostle and High Priest of our confession, even Jesus; who was faithful to him that appointed him." Ask him where he finds the stimulus and power to carry on when the road is rough and his answer is, "Consider him that hath endured such gainsaying of sinners against himself, that ye wax not weary, fainting in your souls." Say to him that the world is going to the dogs, that mankind is stupid, brutal, uncivilized, incorrigible, and he says, True enough! "We do not yet see all things controlled by man; what we do see is Jesus."

Some kinds of Christianity I can get on very well without. What relevance have they to a man's problems, trying to live a strong and decent life in a time like this? But Christ himself— my soul! if he could get at us, live in us, shape our thought and our behavior by his spirit, that would make all the difference in the world.

The upshot of this matter comes close home to our present need. The coming of Jesus, prophetic, historically influential, personally moving, is a very reassuring fact too. Heaven knows we need reassurance! Reviewing this last war, we are appalled at the physical destructiveness involved. The hideous facts brought out in the Nuremberg trial, the hideous fact that even before the atomic bomb a hundred thousand civilians were burned to death in one night's raid on Tokyo, the fact that civilians killed by raids on Hamburg outnumber those slain in Hiroshima or Nagasaki—such facts are fearful in their prophecy of physical ruin, unless man changes his ways. But to those, too, who care about man's character quite as much as they care about man's body, the facts are frightening. Dr. Urey, one of our foremost atomic scientists, said this last week: "The morals of the human race have degenerated in an unbelievable way in the last five years. It is not to be expected that they would not further degenerate in a future war."

In all confused eras such as this, what does human nature do? It always looks, not so much for some thing as for some one to believe in. So Germany believed in Hitler and said, He is the answer! So Italy believed in Mussolini and said, He is the answer! We say that people believe in imperialism, nationalism, democracy, communism, and all the rest. Granted! We need not belittle the importance of these abstract beliefs. But we never get to the bottom of the matter until we see how inevitably we humans believe at last, not in isms but in incarnations. It is they who make abstractions real and powerful.

Remember Marshal Foch's saying, "It was not an army that crossed the Alps; it was Hannibal."

Christmas means this at least: a personality has come into the world concerning whom millions believe that he is the answer. Even Paul never said, I know what I have believed. The mystery of life so deep, the confusion of the world so great, he sometimes did not know what he believed. What Paul said went deeper: "I know him whom I have believed." That is Christianity! I wish I could persuade someone here who never has accepted it, to accept it now. I am not inviting you to sign a theological creed on the dotted line. I am not inviting you to join a sectarian denomination, and subscribe to its peculiarities. I am inviting you to see Christ, his revelation of God, his basic principles, his way of life, his spirit and quality, and so seeing him, to say, He is the answer! Cannot we see whither the contrary answers are plunging the whole world now? He is the answer! That is the everlasting truth!

The Most Thrilling Rescue Story in the World *

NOTHING is so thrilling as a rescue story. Sometime since a private soldier badly wounded in the South Pacific and hospitalized home, was still trying to discover the name of a corporal who had saved his life. In a desperate situation, all hope gone, this corporal, whom in his agony the soldier did not recognize, crawled to his help, carried him to safety, and disappeared. Who was he? the soldier wants to know, for nothing goes deeper with us and takes hold harder than the experience of sacrificial saviorhood when the need is deep.

During that last week of the Master's life in Jerusalem two symbols stand out—palm branches and the cross. The palm branches represent the acclaim of shouting crowds, greeting a Messiah coming to his own; the cross represents tragedy. Why did not Christianity take the palm branch as its symbol, a joyful token to be happy over, with its recollections of hosannas to the conquering Christ? Yet we know well that the Christian church would never have survived the centuries with only a palm branch over its high altar. The cross goes deeper— much deeper!—deeper than anything else into the heart of man's experience—need and deliverance; a rescue story; sin and saviorhood there on Calvary, locked in desperate encounter, with the fate of the world depending on which of those two in the end shall win.

The central issue of history is this struggle between sin and saviorhood, and the cross of Christ is the climactic exhibition of them both. There on Calvary one sees appalling sin, rejecting and slaying the divinest personality that ever came to earth. Yet there on Calvary one also sees sacrificial saviorhood, the supreme rescue story in man's history, one who did not need

* A Palm Sunday Sermon.

to do it voluntarily taking on himself the burden of the world's iniquity that he might deliver men and blaze the trail for a kingdom of righteousness on earth. That is life, the real thing and no fooling, this desperate struggle between sin at its worst and saviorhood at its best.

This should be real to us now. Behind this outward war we have been fighting is a deeper war that no military victory will settle, a war not simply between nations but within nations, and within every individual life—sin against saviorhood, and saviorhood against sin. Who now, looking at this world, can doubt the reality of that struggle? Mankind needs a rescue story, saviorhood that can grapple with this sin of ours and overthrow it. Of that tremendous encounter between devilishness and deliverance the cross is the symbol—both there, sin at its darkest, and saviorhood at its best. So from the beginning to the end of the New Testament Jesus is called savior, "Our Savior, Jesus Christ." We have become used to that, but it is nothing to become used to. Those first Christians thought of him in terms of the redeeming thing he did as vividly as that soldier thinks of the corporal who delivered him from death. Christ, to them, was the thrilling center of a rescue story.

One of the first things that this struggle between sin and saviorhood says to us, is, Don't oversimplify your philosophy of life! We all are tempted to do that, to seek some neat formula that will smooth out, at least in theory, life's disharmonies and conflicts and help us to forget them. Men, for example, adopt a Browningesque optimism, saying,

> "God's in his heaven—
> All's right with the world!"

and so go on to say that evil is not real, but only the shadow cast by good. As the rising sun is real, so is goodness, they say, but all the evil of the world is but the passive, transient shade which some temporary obstacle casts as the sun rises.

That is a childish philosophy! Sin is no mere shadow cast by good, but a demonic, devastating power. It can incarnate itself in a moral maniac who plunges the whole world into such collective agony as mankind has never, in all its history, endured before.

Or men get at this false sense of cheerful harmony in life by working out elaborate philosophies, baptizing evolution with optimism and saying—believe it or not, Herbert Spencer did say this—"Progress . . . is not an accident, but a necessity." That too is a childish philosophy. We are not predestinated to progress. We do evolve socially into the possession of such scientific power as men never had before, and then diabolical sin lays hold on that power and with it civilization may yet commit suicide. We do evolve socially into a world neighborhood, and then pride and selfishness corrupt all the new contacts and propinquities until the more the possibilities of brotherhood are here, the more the actualities of hatred, prejudice and war are terrible.

Such oversimplified philosophies will no longer do. The Devil is real. I do not mean, of course, that he is an individual, with horns and a tail; he is much worse than that—the symbol of a positive, devastating force in history that can destroy every human hope. Such is the realistic fact, and if it were the only fact pessimism would be the consequence. So Gibbon saw history as "little more than the register of the crimes, follies, and misfortunes of mankind."

Holy Week brings us another message, a stirring message. All that Gibbon saw in history—crime, folly, misfortune—is here, but something else is here too, saviorhood, voluntarily assuming the burden of the world's needs and redeeming men. The central fact of history is no easygoing harmony but this fierce conflict on which the whole outcome of our human adventure depends—saviorhood against sin.

The story runs that when things were at their worst during the Civil War, hopelessness rampant and Lincoln besmeared with every kind of calumny and abuse, a friend said to him, "Why not resign, and let them sink or swim?" And Lincoln slowly and sadly answered, "If I resign, they perish." How did Gibbon miss that factor in history—spirits who will not resign, but shouldering the burden of the world, that they do not need to shoulder, take up their cross and deliver men?

Let us say it to ourselves this Palm Sunday as we see the Master entering Jerusalem amid the crowd's hosannas—saviorhood is in this world. Darkest Africa, but the David Livingstones too; devastating diseases, but the Pasteurs and their successors too; appalling ignorance, but the Horace Manns and their colleagues too; the Devil and all his representatives, but Christ too. Lowly and riding on an ass's foal he came to the great city, a savior, and there he faced sin as all saviors do—the sin of ecclesiastics who did not wish their orthodox establishment disturbed, of businessmen wanting no money changers' tables overturned to their profit's hurt, of politicians like Caiaphas playing their clever, selfish games, of cowards like Pilate washing his hands of his responsibility, of Roman soldiers doing whatever cruelty they were commanded, of the crowd persuaded by skillful propaganda to cry, "Crucify him!" So, as always, saviorhood faced sin, but today, nearly two thousand years afterwards, it's not the sin we are celebrating, but the saviorhood. Thank God, that is in the world!

Because the central fact of history is this struggle between sin and saviorhood never expect Christianity to pipe down on the reality and terribleness of sin. So long as Christianity is here at all it will be insisting on sin's reality, its power and its catastrophe. Where, for example, is intellectual dishonesty most clearly seen as an evil, and most insistently hated? You had better go to a scientific laboratory for that, for in a scientific laboratory the eyes of men are centered on a great good, indispensable to the progress of the truth—intellectual honesty, objective, disinterested, uncompromising. It is there that the curse of intellectual dishonesty would be most strongly felt and hated. So not in the

dives and dens and moral slums of life is sin best understood
and its diabolical reality most powerfully felt, but in the gospel
of Christ, for there the central struggle of human life stands out,
no oversimplified Pollyanna philosophy but the real truth—a
great conflict, sin against saviorhood, and saviorhood against
sin.

Consider further that all deep understanding of Christ's meaning depends on seeing this. It is easy to make a hero of Jesus,
as though that category could sum up his meaning. Well, he is
a hero! It is easy to describe Jesus as a spiritual genius; his
profound influence on human thought suggests that category.
Well, he is a genius! It is easy to make an ideal of him; his
personal quality, far ahead of us like a pillar of cloud by day
and of fire by night, suggests that category. Well, he is the ideal!
But when we have called him hero, genius, ideal, or what you
will, we must go far beyond that if we are to apprehend his
meaning. He is Savior, the heart and center of a rescue story.

So to the Jews, Moses is a hero, a genius, an ideal. But ask
the Jews why all these centuries his name has been their stimulus
and strength, and this profounder fact emerges—a slave people
in Egypt, hopeless under Pharaoh's tyranny, were emancipated
by a savior. What a thrilling experience that is, familiar in our
day, as hapless folk long imprisoned in Philippine concentration camps know well, who have heard the incredible good
tidings that a deliverer has come!

This Holy Week celebrates that exciting truth at the heart
of the Christian gospel. There is saviorhood in this world, and
in it is a quality which, really seen, lays hold on us as nothing
else ever does. In a rural section of southern California, we are
told, a Mexican mother died, leaving a family of eight children.
The oldest girl, not yet seventeen, was a tiny thing and upon
her frail shoulders fell the burden of caring for the family. The
neighbors watched her as, taking up the task with courage,
she kept the children clean, well fed, and in school. One day a

friend complimented her on her achievement and she replied, "I can't take any credit for something I have to do." "But, my dear," said the friend, "you don't have to. You could get out of it." The girl paused for a moment, and said, "Yes, that's true. But what about the *have to* that's inside of me?" So! The *have to* that is inside of me! All saviorhood starts there.

Florence Nightingale need not have gone to nurse the wounded in the Crimean War; no outward pressure urged her on; all the circumstances were against her going, the military authorities themselves dubious or antagonistic, and her own family calling her crazy for even thinking of it. But there was that *have to* inside of her. We had better be grateful when we think of this, for all the background of our lives is full of it and every decent and lovely thing we have or hope for has come from it—men and women who need not have done what they did, but who were compelled by a *have to* inside of them.

Ah, Christ, you had that! It was that which took you to the cross. "I lay down my life . . . No man taketh it from me, but I lay it down of myself." "Greater love hath no man than this, that a man lay down his life for his friends." What a "have to" inside of him! So human life is a struggle between sin—whatever debases and debauches life—and the great succession of the saviors, with the "have to" inside of them. On which side of that issue are we? Let no one spend this Holy Week without facing that question! In one of Rembrandt's paintings of the crucifixion, one's eyes naturally rest at first upon the central figures in the scene; but by and by, in the shadows, one sees another figure— Rembrandt, himself—no doubt about it—Rembrandt himself, helping to crucify Christ. In a world whose central fact is the struggle between sin and saviorhood, on the wrong side of the issue!

Thus our thought brings us inevitably a further step to an intimate personal matter. This struggle between sin and saviorhood is going on inside every one of us. When we say "sin" we are not meaning little, trivial matters, but the gigantic forces of destructive evil that corrupt and devastate the world. Look what sin is doing to humanity today, this most tragic Holy Week mankind ever spent, with such barbarity let loose and such chaos following it as earth never before staggered under. And just as all the goodness in human life must first of all be goodness inside people, one by one, so all the sin in human life is first of all evil inside men's souls. This awful spectacle that now confronts us is like a moving picture on a vast screen, but back of it are the small films, the incredibly small films, of individual people in whom the picture has its origin and its explanation, the world's sin only the enlargement of personal sin. We cannot thrust off this struggle of sin against saviorhood and saviorhood against sin as though it were public only; it is private, the central issue of each person's life. As another put it, "No possible rearrangement of bad eggs can ever make a good omelet."

After many years of personal counselling, do not tell me that the Devil, in the sense we mean, is not real in individual experience. See what he does! He approaches a man, saying, Come on, be free; don't be a slave, be free! And a man follows him, free to do as he pleases, until one day he wakes up to the ghastly fact that he is no longer free to stop. Lured by the bait of freedom he has landed in the trap of habit, and the classic words of William James about the man who kept saying, "I won't count this time!" come true. "He may not count it," says James, "and a kind Heaven may not count it; but it is being counted none the less. Down among his nerve-cells and fibres the molecules are counting it, registering and storing it up to be used against him when the next temptation comes." Believe me, the power of sin to become habitual is dreadfully real!

Or, again, the Devil says to a man, Here is a pleasure; come on, enjoy it! To be sure, it's wrong, but you can get away with it. What is life for, if not to enjoy yourself? So the man follows him, fascinated in expectation by the indulgence that he plans.

But then the day comes when the evil passes from anticipation, through committal into memory, and something momentous happens, as the sense of guilt takes hold, settles down, will not let go. Then like a bell buoy on a lonely ocean, tolled by the restless sea, remorse tolls in the man's unquiet soul and will not be stilled. When one deals with real sin, how different the retrospect can be from the prospect!

Or, again, the Devil says to a man, Be yourself! Why this sense of responsibility for everybody else? Live your own life; do as you please! So the man follows him, does as he pleases, and then the day comes when the consequences begin to fall— not upon himself alone, on someone else, his family, his children, his friends. If only he could keep the consequences of his sin within the confines of his own life and face them there himself, alone! But he cannot. Always the innocent suffer for our sins.

This thing we are talking about is true to our experience. The sin that ruins the world roots back into the sins we personally consent to, and about the whole duty of man is first to accept saviorhood for himself—forgiveness, cleansing, re-established fellowship with God, divine resources of moral power; and, then, to join the saving forces in the world, the men and women with a compelling "have to" inside of them.

The one thing that makes it worth while preaching this sermon is that that dual experience—accepting saviorhood for ourselves and then going out to be saviors—could happen here now to some of us. It had better happen to a lot of people, for, friends, we cannot take the civilized securities of human life for granted any more—not any more! We have been doing that through many an optimistic decade—taking civilization for granted. Of course, civilization! As one expected the sun to rise on the morrow, so one expected civilization. But look now at this vast catastrophe and collapse! Now it is going to be a struggle, the most fateful struggle in human history—sin against saviorhood, and saviorhood against sin—and the saviors must first of all be saved themselves, as Moses met God alone at the burning bush before he confronted Pharaoh in the public court. So may some of us this week face the cross of Christ, and seeing there sin and saviorhood locked in that desperate encounter, choose—choose Christ's side!

An Unavoidable Choice Faces Our Jerusalem Too*

AS JERUSALEM confronts Christ that week before Easter long ago, one fact stands plainly out: what a relief it would have been if they had not had to confront him! The city as a whole did not want to accept him; they did not want to crucify him; if only they could have dodged the issue and done nothing about him, what a relief! The inside of Pilate's mind will always be a puzzle but surely this factor was present: he wished he could avoid responsibility. Accepting Christ was preposterous, crucifying Christ distasteful—why did he have to do anything with Christ? He even symbolized this desire to side-step decision by publicly washing his hands of the whole matter.

Indeed, Pilate's wife, we are told, sent him an anxious message which ran: "Have thou nothing to do with that righteous man." Most of all, Pilate desired that—to have nothing to do with Christ; free from the whole disturbing business, to make no decision about him. But although he was the Roman procurator and Jesus was a carpenter from Galilee, he stood confronted with an issue he could not dodge. For or against—that he could choose; but what his wife urged on him he could not choose: "Have thou nothing to do with that righteous man."

I Let us begin by recognizing our kinship with Pilate in our instinctive desire to side-step issues. We are all escapists, wanting to run away from difficult decisions, and naturally so, for decision is the hardest work in the world. None may scoff at that Roman procurator, wishing he could retreat into neutrality. What a lotus land that is, to be neither for nor against, but neutral, having nothing to do with some difficult decision!

* A Palm Sunday Sermon.

[203]

But alas! life is not made for neutrals. Life habitually presents us not with three choices—pro, con or indifference—but with two choices, pro or con, one or the other. When Jesus said, "He that is not with me is against me," and again, "He that is not against us is for us," he stated a kind of fact that forever defeats the Pilates, trying to wash their hands of some great matter.

In the psychological realm we face this. Habit, for example—what a nuisance to have to choose between habits! Sobriety or drunkenness, sexual self-control or the lack of it, harnessed temper or explosive anger, Christian altruism or self-centeredness—if one could only be neutral about such matters, what a relief! But something mightier than we are confronts us: "Sow an act and reap a habit; sow a habit and reap a character; sow a character and reap a destiny." Try as we may to wash our hands of the whole matter, one way or another we do become creatures of habit. We must choose.

As in the psychological, so in the social realm we face this. American isolationism was escapism. What a nuisance international interdependence and world government are! What troublesome responsibilities they involve us in! Let's have nothing to do with them, said isolationism. But now the international situation has walked up on us in so imperative a fashion that everyone knows neutrality is out, with not a chance left for any great nation to avoid decision between world government and war.

Palm Sunday dramatized in unforgettable fashion this impossibility of neutrality on great issues. When we read that Jesus "stedfastly set his face to go to Jerusalem," we generally think of what that meant to Jesus, but today we are thinking of what it meant to Jerusalem. If only he had stayed away, what a relief! Why did they have to face that decision which split the city wide open, some welcoming him with hosannas and palm branches and some convinced he must be liquidated? A disturbing nuisance Jesus was, coming thus to Jerusalem, and there is no use trying to keep ourselves out of that picture. Human nature being what it is, Christ is disturbing. We Christians commonly interpret him in terms of his loveliness; we call him glorious names; but he himself said he came to cast fire on the earth. Something incendiary about Jesus starts a conflagration wherever he appears. To our human nature he is upsetting. Why must we be haunted by his ideals so far above us, and made miserable by the necessity of choosing either for him or against? Would not life be easier if he had never come, so to challenge us with his demands?

If that sounds irreverent I appeal to a great Christian theologian of the last century, Kierkegaard, whose influence has powerfully revived in our time because he so forthrightly tells the truth about us: "Let us collect all the New Testaments there are in existence, let us carry them out to an open place or up upon a mountain, and then, while we all kneel down, let some one address God in this fashion: Take this book back again; we men, such as we are now, are no good at dealing with a thing like this, it only makes us unhappy. My proposal is that like the inhabitants of Gadara we beseech Christ to 'depart out of our coasts.'"

A man who has never felt like that about Christ has never, I suspect, taken him seriously. From the difficult decisions he forces on us our human nature gladly would escape. Let us see ourselves so today, in Pilate's shoes, escapists that we are, often trying to have nothing to do with him, while still, after nearly two thousand years, he confronts us, saying, For or against, you must decide.

In every realm there are personalities who so present the world with forced decisions, and they all have this quality—they are the great revealers. Copernicus as an individual could be side-stepped, but when he revealed the truth about the solar system mankind faced an issue where neutrality was impossible: either the sun circled about the earth, or the earth about the sun, one or the other. In the orthodox Moslem University in Cairo a professor some years ago was asked which type of astronomy they taught there, Copernican or pre-Copernican, and he answered, "We teach both." In vain, however, they tried thus to sit undecided on the fence. It is one or the other, and in the long run mankind must be for or against.

So Jesus was more than an individual; he was a revealer. We commonly picture him as teaching ideals, saying, This ought to be so; but what he really said was, This is so, the everlasting truth, the way God's moral order is. The Golden Rule—this is the law of life in God's world; the infinite value of every human soul in the sight of God—this is the truth; good will and brotherhood the precondition of mankind's welfare—this is the eternal fact. If someone here has been thinking that he can be neutral concerning Christ, I answer, Surely we can side-step decision about men whose greatness lies only in their self-centered genius, and can refuse to have anything to do with those who represent nothing beyond themselves, but the great revealers of truth, whether in the physical or spiritual realm, present us with forced decisions. For or against—mankind in the end must take sides.

That Christ is the revealer of eternal truth finds confirmation in a fact to which we Christians too seldom appeal, namely, that so many other seers have said some of the same things that Jesus said. "Whatsoever ye would that men should do to you, do ye even so to them," said Jesus. Yes, and Confucianism says, "Do not unto others what you would not they should do unto you." And Buddhism says, "Hurt not others with that which pains yourself." And Hinduism says, "Do naught to others which if done to thee, would cause thee pain." And Islam says, "No one of you is a believer until he loves for his brother what he loves for himself." And Judaism says, "What is hurtful to yourself do not to your fellow man. That is the whole law and the remainder is but commentary." Strangely enough, some Christians seem to think that this sort of fact detracts from Jesus' uniqueness and originality. Upon the contrary, when eternal truth, waiting to be revealed, breaks through the clouds and is glimpsed and welcomed by many seers, that confirms the revelation. So, long before Copernicus, Pythagoras guessed that the earth circled about the sun. What would you expect? If an everlasting truth is really there, shall not eyes other than one man's get a glimpse of it? Nevertheless it was Copernicus, not Pythagoras, who really confronted the world with what he saw, and it is Christ who supremely forces the issue on us now, saying about one great matter after another, This is the everlasting truth; are you for it or against?

Were Jesus only an individual we could side-step him. Pilate could even kill him as an individual. But the truth he revealed— no nails spiked that to the cross. Pilate little guessed what he was up against when he tried to have nothing to do with him.

To be sure, in one area where Christ's revelation runs many still think they can be neutral: namely, about Jesus' God. They suppose they can be agnostic about him and have nothing to do with him. Well, we can be neutral about God in theory, but the God-question is never seriously faced until, carried out of theory, we confront it in practical life. Every man has his God. A man may give his life to money, alcohol, lust, what you will —but every man has his God. We are born worshipers, always giving our lives to something. Have we not heard Hitler say, "We want no God but Germany"? The God-question is inescapable; no one avoids it. See idolatrous mankind today serving ruinous deities whose worship is the menace of the world, and is it not clear? No man is or can be neutral on the God-question; he chooses either Christ's God or some other. For or against the God and Father of our Lord Jesus Christ—on that issue no convenient fence exists on which, undecided, one can sit. What a troublesome personality Christ is still, as he was in old Jerusalem. If only we could dodge him—but we can't; if only we could have nothing to do with him—but we can't. "He that is not with me is against me."

See how vividly our present crisis in civilization lights up this truth. A long way off seem those youthful days of mine when I had my first struggles about faith in Christ. Those struggles were predominantly theoretical: was this theological statement or that about him the more credible—so ran debate in my troubled mind. That speculative debate has its place; I do not regret it. But now the issue about Christ rises in a form that thrusts all that into the background. Hold this theory or that about him, still there he stands, announcing a way of life for men and nations that this world must choose or else choose its opposite; and the opposite, in all its naked horror and calamity, is so intolerable that I would all mankind could be made to face the issue.

I am not talking about secondary things in Christianity. Many of them matter little, and about them one can be neutral. This theory or that, this ritual or that, this denomination or that—cannot the English king be a Presbyterian in Scotland, and an Episcopalian in England? What difference do such things make? One does not need to choose. But Christ's basic principles and way of life present a forced issue, an inescapable decision; that, or its opposite, we will choose. "Have nothing to do with that righteous man"—so Pilate tried, but alas! for centuries the grim words that curse his memory have been repeated by millions: "Crucified under Pontius Pilate." What a decision he made when he tried not to decide!

Christ is beautiful. I agree.

> "Majestic sweetness sits enthroned
> Upon the Saviour's brow."

Any preacher would prefer to present him only so—the most glorious spirit earth has known, whom to choose is to choose abundant life. From all man's ugliness and cruelty one turns to him today and wonders why the world does not acclaim him with hosannas as God's best gift to man. But there is another side to Christ. He said so himself. Listen to him, speaking of his truth: "He that falleth on this stone shall be broken to pieces: but on whomsoever it shall fall, it will scatter him as dust." So the law of gravitation is marvelous to those who accept and use it well, but misused it is a stone on which men break themselves to pieces. Thus, too, the everlasting truth which Christ reveals is to those that accept it, beautiful, but like all truth, when rejected, it becomes a rock on which men and nations can crash in ruin. The nations have been doing that—are doing it. Pilate did that long ago. He thought he was sitting in judgment on Jesus while all the time Jesus was sitting in judgment on him, and his name and memory have been broken in pieces on that rock. Friends, if this Palm Sunday our Jerusalem is to be represented, not by Pilate, not by the priestly claque that cried, "Crucify him!" in the Praetorium, but by the people in the streets who welcomed him with palm branches and hosannas, then a personal decision is presented to each of us. No man can avoid it. We are for or against.

Consider that personal fact for a moment now for it is the crux of the whole matter. Whenever an individual faced Jesus he faced a decision. Zacchaeus, the tax gatherer, with his dishonest exploitation, confronted in Jesus no theoretical matter he could hem and haw about, plead agnosticism and leave undecided. An ethical choice was presented to him, with yes or no for the answer—would he or would he not make restitution for his ill-gotten gains, and clean up his life? I am pleading with some one here now to go back behind the ecclesiastical Christ whom we often discuss in theory, to face the historic Christ as he confronted men. Dives, mishandling wealth; the woman of Samaria, mishandling sex; the Pharisees, with their race prejudice, hating all Samaritans; Nicodemus, needing to be born again; Pilate, trying to dodge the most critical choice of his life—these and many another the Master faced and always with a forced decision: will you or won't you? If they could have side-stepped him and been neutral, what a relief! But they had to choose.

My sympathy goes out especially to some young people here. You're up against it! You've got to choose! Trying not to choose is the fatalest choice of all. Seeing from the vantage point of elder years the far-off consequence of your decision now, I could almost wish that it were possible to relieve you of that necessity, discover for you, if I could, some safe neutrality to which you could escape, but you too, in the end, will either accept Christ or not. Even though you do not use his name in making your decision, you are up against the kind of life he stood for, the truth that he revealed—for or against that, you will be. Ah Jerusalem, Jerusalem, no ancient city only, but our world now, with Christ coming over the brow of Olivet, to confront you with his claims, God grant for our children's sake a different decision than was given then! Before this world finds peace and happiness, the cry that welcomed him to the city gates must swell to such unanimous accord that all opposing cries are drowned in its greeting, in which may our hearts join today: "Blessed is he that cometh in the name of the Lord: Hosanna in the highest."

The Eternal Victorious Over the Temporal *

WHEN in his letter to the Corinthians Paul wrote, "The things which are seen are temporal; but the things which are not seen are eternal," he stated the proposition on which faith in immortality rests. The first part of his statement is beyond doubt—everything visible passes away. To us as children life looked secure and our plans reached down a long, long road that seemed to have no ending but, growing older, we awoke to the insecurity of mortal life. Someone whom we loved died; we read biography—how young Shelley sang songs more winsome than his own *Skylark*, when a squall of wind off the Italian coast ended his melody. We began to understand Shakespeare's lines:

> "All the world's a stage,
> And all the men and women merely players:
> They have their exits and their entrances."

Moreover, life's transiency concerns not individuals alone but societies and nations. When first we thought of them, how secure they seemed! But Egypt, Babylon, Assyria, Greece, Rome, vast and stable, were in the end like sand houses on the shore which tides of destiny, moved by a higher heaven than man's hands can reach, rose up and swept away.

Even with nations this sense of transiency cannot stop. The successive generations of men, like snowstorms, multitudinous in flakes, fall on the earth only to melt and disappear. As children, death seemed strange to us, but as we grew older wars came, and news of famine and pestilence, and we perceived that death, like a reaper, mows millions down. Is some one here today eighty years old? Since you were born between two and

* An Easter Sermon.

three billion people have died. Martineau's prayer gains new significance as we grow older: "O God, . . . before whose face the generations rise and pass away."

Even here, however, the sense of transiency cannot stop. We call the stars eternal, but they are not eternal. Some of them in embryo are being born out of whirling nebulae; some are in their fierce and fiery youth; some, like our own sun, are past middle age; and some are growing old and soon will die. Everything seen is temporal—ourselves, our nations, the generations, the very stars.

Against this background it seems strange to hear some say, What difference does it make whether one believes in immortality? What difference! How can a thoughtful man face the transiency of the universe and all within it and not ask himself, Is there nothing that lasts? Is it all a passing shadow show leaving not a wrack behind? Is this first superficial description we just have given of it the final word? Then in this vast changefulness there is no permanence at all. The very thought of that makes a man hungry for something eternal. There must be something here that lasts, some strand of abiding unity upon which the changes all are strung; else, as William James said, this whole creation were no better than a silly moving picture film that might as well be run backward as forward, because it means nothing either way. We must not believe in a senseless universe like that if we can help it. Our Easter thought is serious business. We are pleading for the presence somewhere of something that abides.

As a matter of fact, almost everyone believes that there is something here that lasts. Some turn Paul's text upside down and say: The things which are seen are eternal, but the things which are not seen are temporal. They mean that the physical universe goes on forever; these special stars pass but new ones come; these solar universes die but others take their places. Personality, they think, passes away and is no more; spiritual life, love, character, honor, beauty—these, the thin fragrance of matter finely organized, are blown away and perish utterly. Only omnipotent matter crashes victoriously on its endless course. This, my friends, is what it means to deny immortality. There is something here that lasts, the deniers say, but it is the lowest that endures, the physical eternal, while the spiritual dies.

Here is evident the momentous meaning of the Easter message, proclaiming to all the world a gospel upon whose truth our best hopes depend, that not the lowest but the highest persists, spiritual life abiding, things seen, temporal, but things not seen, eternal.

Consider, to begin with, what deep meaning this message puts into the universe. Materialism oversimplifies even the physical cosmos, for there too the profoundest forces are unseen. Planets are marvelous, but not so marvelous as the invisible gravitation that holds them all together. Stars are wonderful, but not so wonderful as the invisible mathematical formulae in accordance with which they are organized. The creative Power from which all things come, no man ever saw, but it weaves the fabric of everything that is. Even this physical cosmos, where all the seen comes from the unseen, is a thousand times more mysterious than materialists guess.

This marvel deepens when one thinks of living things. Amid the lofty Alps one stands thunderstruck at the towering peaks, thrusting their heads up into heaven, their shoulders caped with snow; and then to rest his eyes from this magnificence he looks down at the blue forget-me-nots, growing along the glacier's edge. Pick one of them, tiny, frail, perishable, yet one of them is more marvelous than all the Alps. For the Alps are dead, but this has life. They have been thrust up from without, but this developed from within. They stand static for centuries but this grows, and dies, and is reborn from seeds that it creates. Here is the real marvel of the universe—life, that no man ever yet has seen or been able to explain, in comparison with which the Alpine peaks are a simple thing.

Well, then, pick up not a forget-me-not but a little child, and is not he more marvelous than all the stars? For he lives, but they are dead. He thinks, but they do not even know they are thought about. He loves, but the rumors of it never reach them. He achieves character, but they never can. The stars do not meditate upon their transiency but even a child has dreams of life to come, and thinks he was not made to die. Surely, spiritual life is the supreme marvel and treasure of creation.

This, then, is at stake on Easter Day: Is this a universe that keeps its lowest and lets its highest go? Some people think we Christians believe in immortality because we clamorously insist upon the selfish continuance of our individual lives. How absurd! Who among us is sufficiently obsessed by his own importance to insist upon his going on forever, if that is all that is involved? What we are profoundly concerned about is the kind of creation we are living in. Is it a universe that saves its lowest, clinging to dust with tenacious eagerness and with careless fingers throwing spirit all away? What an irrational world! Suppose you had a magnificent house, and suppose that through the halls and up the stairs and around the galleries of that house there played a child, your child, and suppose that some day fire threatened and you had to choose which you would keep, your house or your child. If you chose to keep the house and lose the child, we should know you to be as insane as you are wicked, as wicked as you are insane. Well, is this an insane universe, that keeps the house and lets the children go, that clings to matter and cares not for spirit, that hugs dust and throws soul away? As Professor Palmer of Harvard said about his wife's death, who can fail to feel the irrationality of the universe "if out of deference to a few particles of disordered matter it excludes so fair a spirit?" Thank God for the Easter message, affirming that God's world is not thus mad, but that while the physical passes, the spiritual endures!

Consider not only the meaning this puts into the universe but the light it throws upon the nature of immortality itself. The details of life after death we cannot imagine. As Reinhold Niebuhr said, it is unwise for Christians to claim any knowledge of either the furniture of heaven or the temperature of hell. Of course it is! Paul, for one, never indulged in such folly, but when he summed up his thoughts of the world to come, cried, "Eye hath not seen, nor ear heard, neither have entered into the heart of man, the things which God hath prepared for them that love him." That is to say, immortality is a great adventure into the unseen and the unknown. Remember Peter Pan standing on the rock in the midst of the lagoon, while the waters rose about him until drowning seemed inevitable? "To die," cried Peter, "to die will be an awfully big adventure!"

Many people need this emphasis on death as an adventure. Faith in immortality, they think, is meant for the weak, to comfort them in feebleness; it is an opiate that makes death hurt less. That is a strange perversion of our actual experience. At any rate, when I, for one, am weak, I care least about immortality. When I am weak, I am willing to lie down, go to sleep and never wake. In hours of weakness I understand what Swinburne felt when he thanked

> "with brief thanksgiving
> Whatever gods may be
> That no life lives forever;
> That dead men rise up never;
> That even the weariest river
> Winds somewhere safe to sea."

When we are weak we feel like that! But when we are strong, when the tides of life are mighty in us, when love powerfully insists on the deathless value of our friends, when possibilities open up within us too fine and deep for threescore years and ten ever to unfold, when we are at our best, it is then we crave the chance of going on. Faith in immortality is not the child of human feebleness seeking an opiate; it springs from human strength pounding against the too narrow bars of our mortality.

When the archeologists first began their investigations of ancient Roman cemeteries, they found everywhere tombstones with seven letters on them: NFFNSNC. These letters represented an old inscription, so familiar that the Romans put only the initials down, and these are the Latin words for which the initials stood: Non fui, fui, non sum, non curo. And this is the translation: I was not, I was, I am not, I do not care. So sons buried fathers, and fathers sons; wives interred husbands, and husbands wives; and over their graves, this cynical, hopeless summary of life was put: I was not, I was, I am not, I do not care. Do you call that an expression of strength? Is it not the quintessence of surrender? Over against those ancient Roman cemeteries, put just one Christian grave, Dean Alford's, who wrote,

> "Ten thousand times ten thousand
> In sparkling raiment bright."

He lies buried in Canterbury, England, and on his grave are inscribed these words: "The inn of a traveler on his road to Jerusalem."

For lack of this emphasis upon adventurousness in our thought of life after death, many come not only to doubt immortality but not really to desire it. Who wants to go to the conventional heaven? It would be intolerable. No live man could stand it for a week! Say to that grammar school son of yours with an earnest and aspiring mind, You can go on forever and forever being a grammar school pupil. Annihilation would be far better. But say to him, You can graduate from grammar school to high school, from high school to college, and from college to life. Always there will be new modes of thinking and new opportunities to learn, and when at last you fall on sleep like Goethe, crying, "More light!" more light will be waiting beyond your power to guess. Minds can grow, spirits can expand, life can move into new dimensions, personality can mount from plane to plane of being beyond the reach of our imaginations' fingertips. That is gospel, not for the feeble, but for the strong, the courageous, the venturesome, who trust God enough to "greet the unseen with a cheer." Do you believe *that* this morning, that God will never let the best in this universe, spiritual life, slip through his fingers, but will always give it infinite opportunity to expand and grow? Believe it! For unless one can think this universe to be utterly insane, it is true: the things seen, temporal, but the things not seen, eternal.

Come further now and see the light this throws upon the special Easter message that Jesus is alive. Once, when accumulating troubles were disturbing Martin Luther, his friends saw him writing with his fingers on the dust of a table top: "Vivit, vivit"—he lives, he lives. Let us say it to ourselves this morning: Christ is alive! Some here may have been disturbed by what we just have said about our inability to know details concerning life to come. They still are curious; they urgently wish they knew. But of course we cannot. How can an unborn babe picture the world he is going to be born into? Nevertheless, from adventuring into an unknown world, many shrink. They are afraid of death. We are not all daring Columbuses, eager to slip our caravels loose from a friendly coast and send them out upon an unknown sea. Turn again, then, to the Easter message. One great thing we do know about the future world—we know who is there. Some spiritual lives whom we have loved make it homelike today, and most of all, he is there, whom Easter celebrates.

In this audience now there may be some young lad whose

mother lives far out upon the western plains. She has never seen New York. Until you came here she thought little of it, but now she thinks of it much of the time. What is New York to her? Not the town of skyscrapers and thronging multitudes, but most of all the place where you are, all else dim except the vivid thought that you are here. And were she to cross the continent, one song would be singing in her heart all the way— not the thought of outward grandeur but the thought of seeing you, where you live.

If someone says that that, like all human analogies, cannot possibly be adequate to fit the circumstances of life to come— too childlike, too simple—I answer, Granted! Yet consider: centuries before Jesus, Plato the philosopher believed in immortality—his *Phaedo* still one of the most magnificent memorials of faith in life eternal man ever wrote—and what Plato meant by it stands clearly out when he says that he would gladly die often to have a chance to talk with Hesiod and Homer. Well, we do not know details about the life to come. Right! Even John Bunyan says that when Pilgrim came within sight of the eternal city he tried to look at it through his glass but his hands shook so that he could not clearly see. We do know something, however—granting life immortal, we know who is there. Lives we loved once were among us here, the seen in them temporal, too temporal and too soon fled; but the unseen in them—we cannot believe *that* will have no end but the grave. And as the years pass and the majority of our friends slip over into the world unseen, the world unseen becomes populous and inviting.

Friends, I appeal to you this Easter morning. You do not really believe that this is so irrational a universe that it keeps the physical forever and lets the spiritual go. Deeper than your doubts is your invincible surmise that death must somehow be an open door through which the unseen and eternal in us pass into life abiding. Science says that all the physical in us is ninety-eight cents worth of chemical material. Is that the last word about us? And when we lift our thought to him through whom the Divine so gloriously shone, can you believe that as the last word about him—ninety-eight cents worth of chemical material, and when that dissolved, all was gone? No! The deeper difficulty lies not in believing in immortality but in disbelieving it, in reducing the imperishable values of the spirit in us to perishable dust. This mortal must put on immortality. Let that faith this Easter morning dignify our lives, ground our characters on unshakable foundations, devote our service to abiding aims, and keep our hope invincible. Hallelujah! The Lord God Omnipotent reigneth!